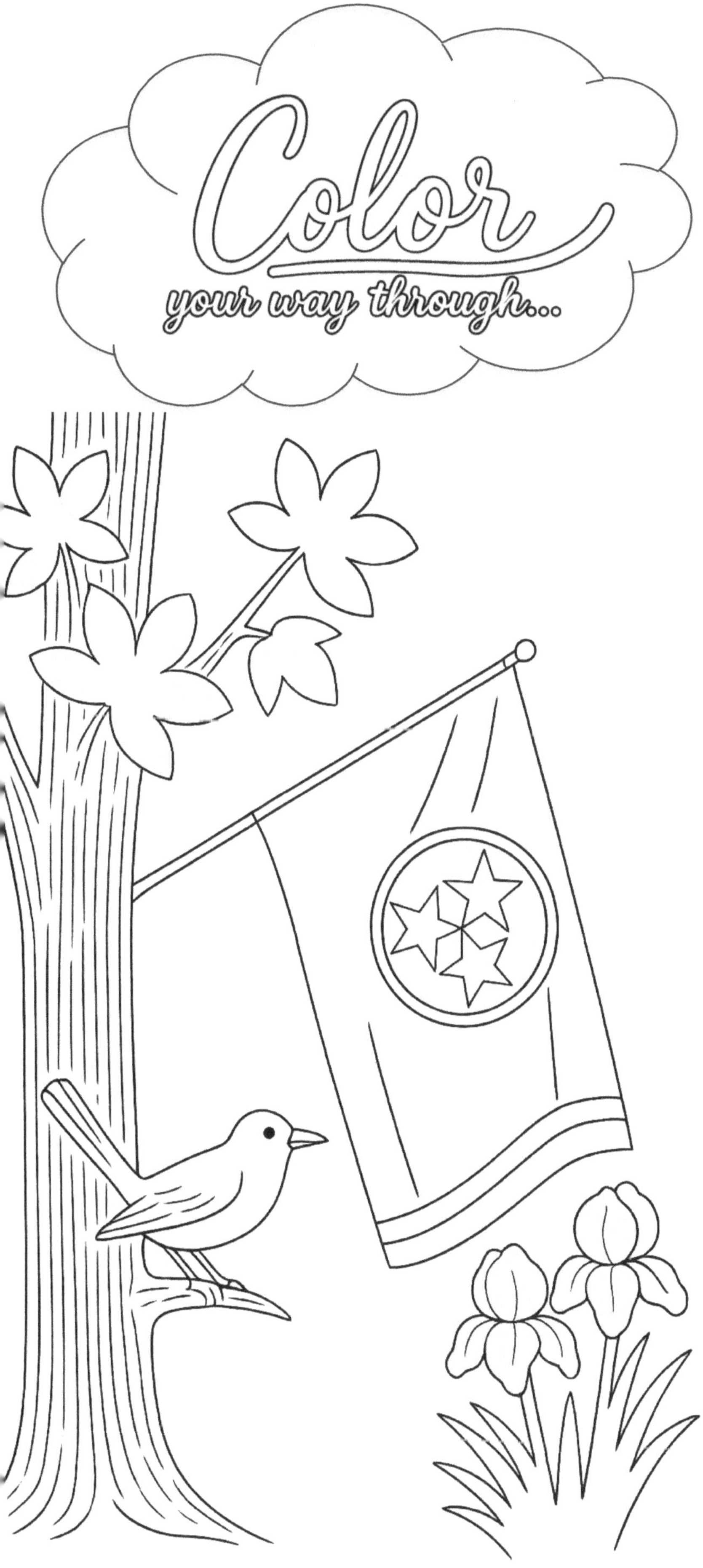

Inspiration for the Book
Each illustration began as a photograph captured while driving through picturesque Franklin and Leiper's Fork, Tennessee. Every image represents a real moment, preserved in lines so you can bring it to life in your own way. Scan the QR code on each page to learn more about the featured location, animal, or local history.

Artistic Credits
Illustrations created and adapted from original photography by LM Gulick. All artwork designed in Franklin, Tennessee. Special thanks for Amy Elrite for the back cover maps.

Permissions & Acknowledgments
All photographs were taken from publicly accessible areas throughout Franklin and Leiper's Fork, Tennessee. Every effort has been made to respect private property and community landmarks. Any recognizable locations or establishments featured are included as artistic representations celebrating the beauty of the region. If you are the owner of a property depicted and have concerns, please contact info@ColorYourWayThrough.store.

About the Creator
LM Gulick is a local photographer and creative storyteller based in Franklin, Tennessee. Her work celebrates Southern charm, small-town heritage, and the beauty hidden in everyday scenes. Through her *Color Your Way Through* series, she invites readers to slow down, explore, and reconnect with the places that make the world around them unforgettable.

Connect
Website: www.ColorYourWayThrough.store
Instagram: @ColorYourWayThrough
Facebook: ColorYourWayThrough
Email: info@ColorYourWayThrough.store

Dedication
This book is dedicated to my children, Aubree, Ainslee, and Lance, for watching for cars while I pulled to the side of the road over and over and over again to snap a photo…
I love you each more than photos can tell!

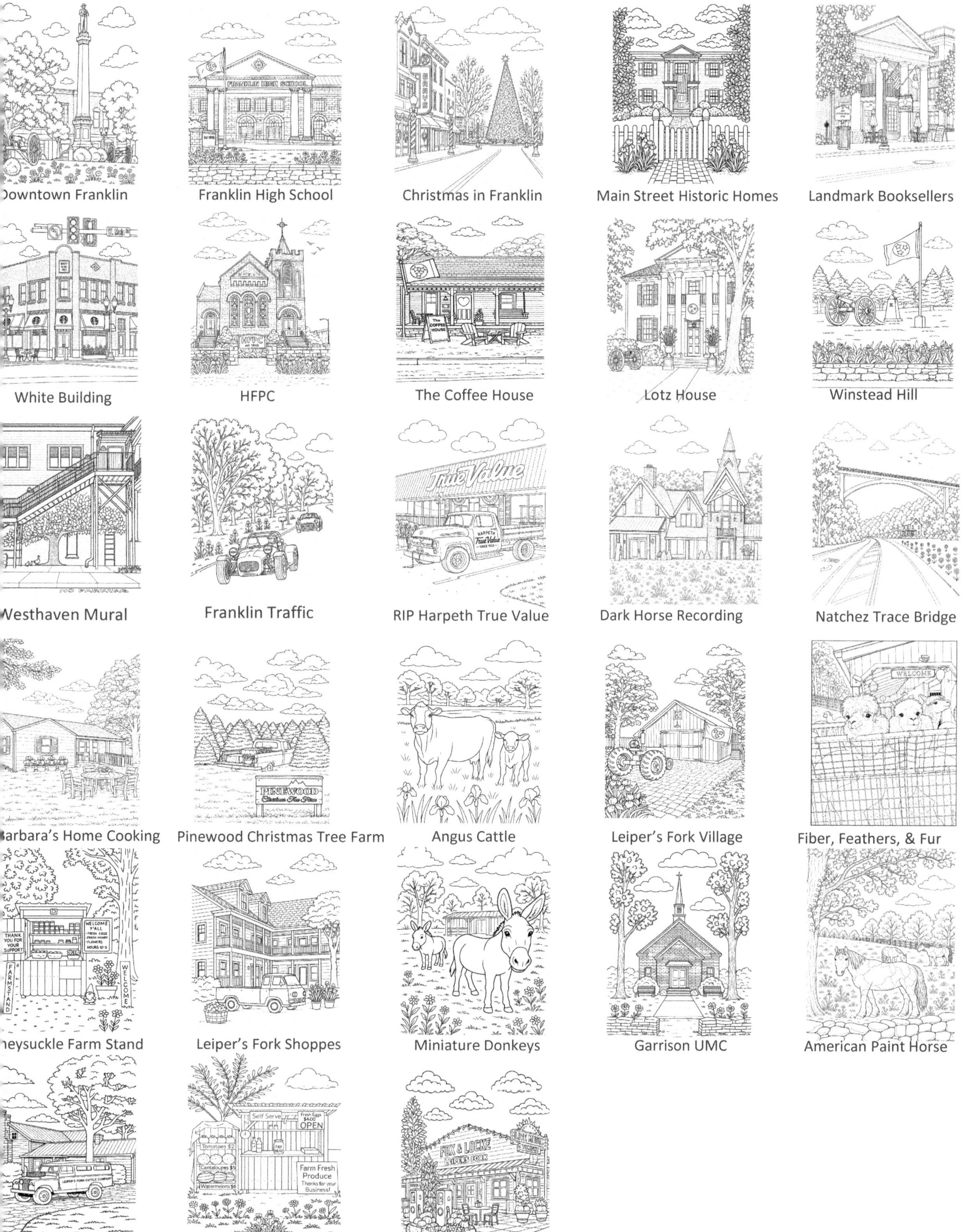

Downtown Franklin
Franklin High School
Christmas in Franklin
Main Street Historic Homes
Landmark Booksellers
White Building
HFPC
The Coffee House
Lotz House
Winstead Hill
Westhaven Mural
Franklin Traffic
RIP Harpeth True Value
Dark Horse Recording
Natchez Trace Bridge
Barbara's Home Cooking
Pinewood Christmas Tree Farm
Angus Cattle
Leiper's Fork Village
Fiber, Feathers, & Fur
Honeysuckle Farm Stand
Leiper's Fork Shoppes
Miniature Donkeys
Garrison UMC
American Paint Horse
LFCC
Logans Farmstand
Fox & Locke

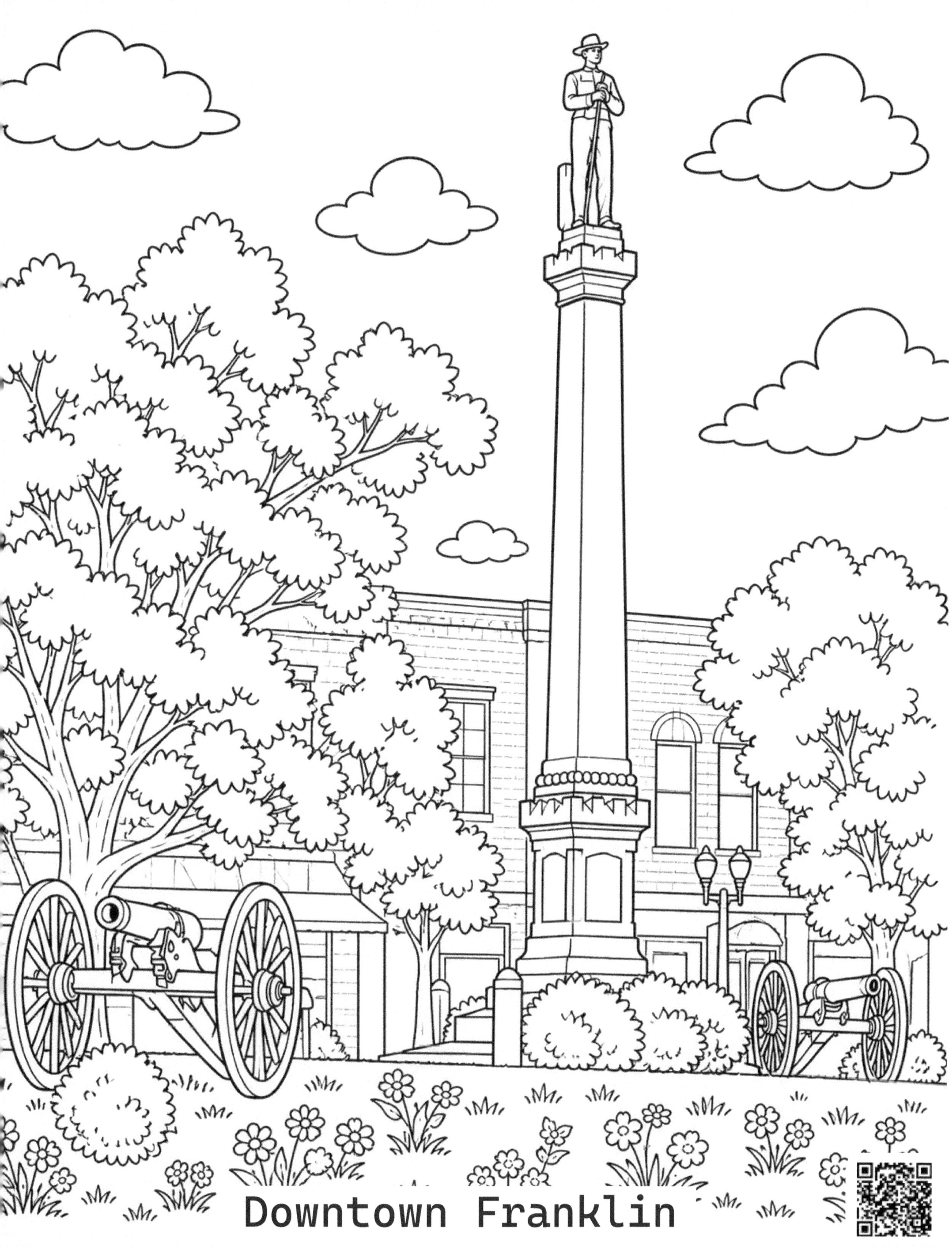

Downtown Franklin

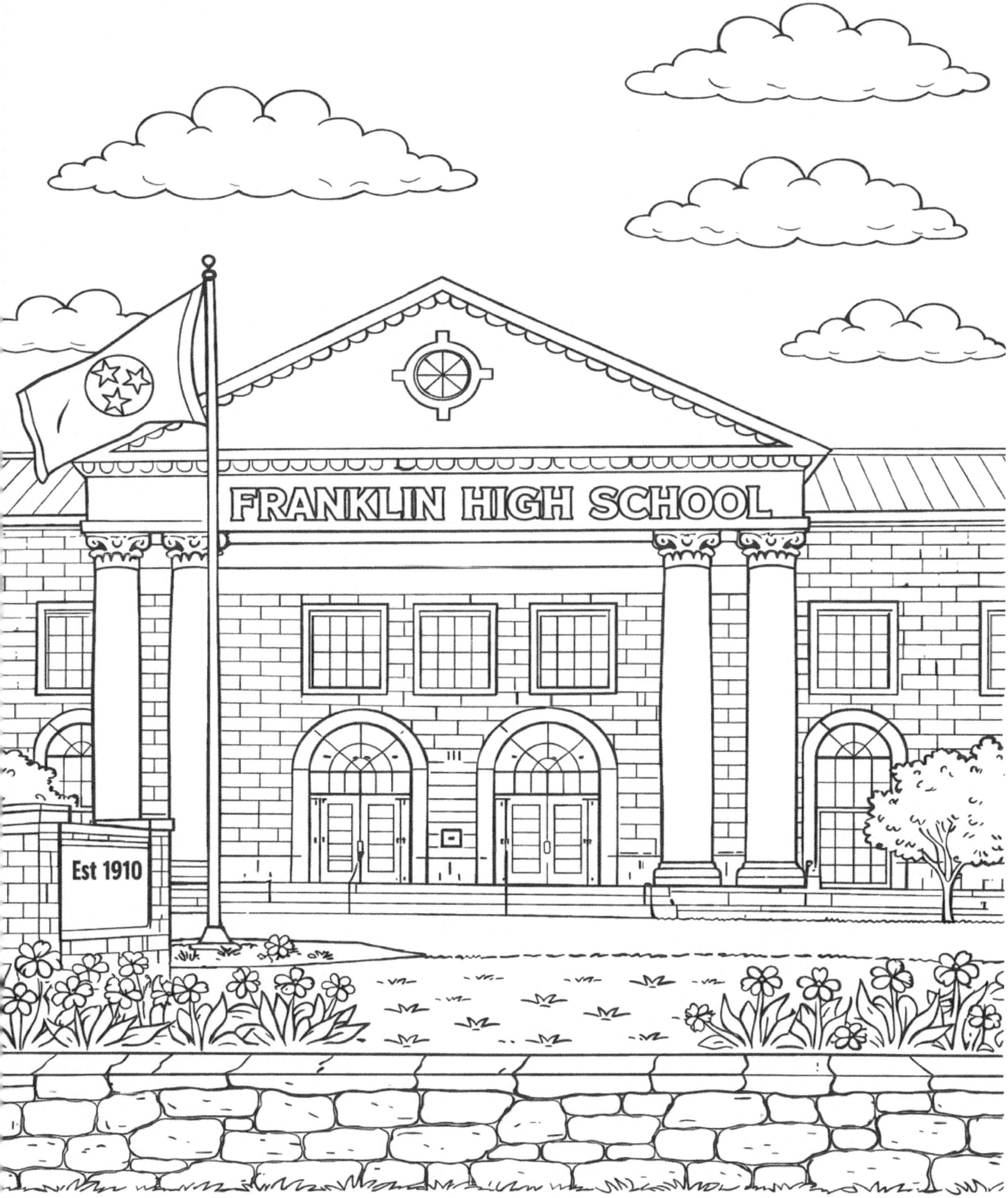

Franklin High School

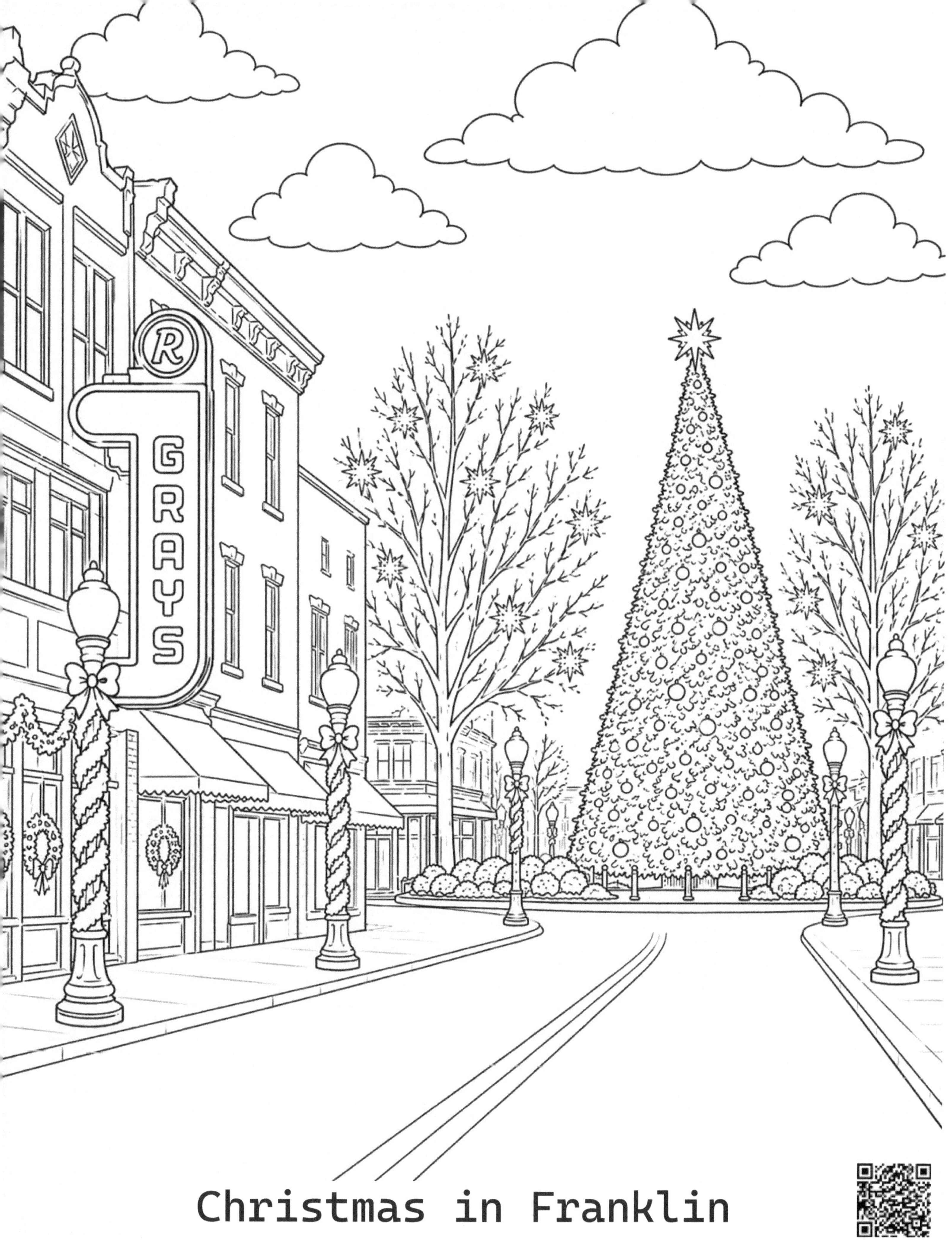

GRAYS
R
Christmas in Franklin

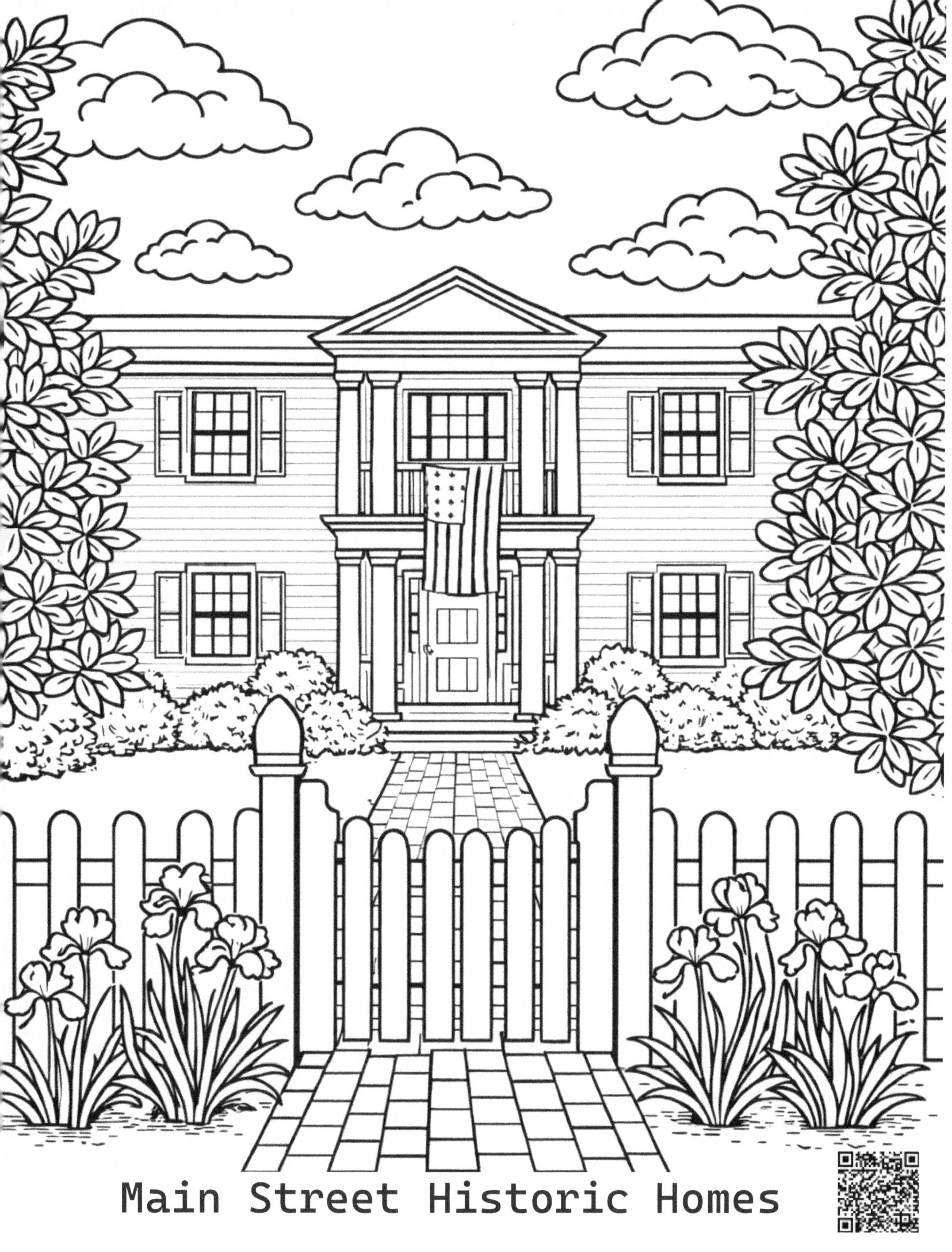

Main Street Historic Homes

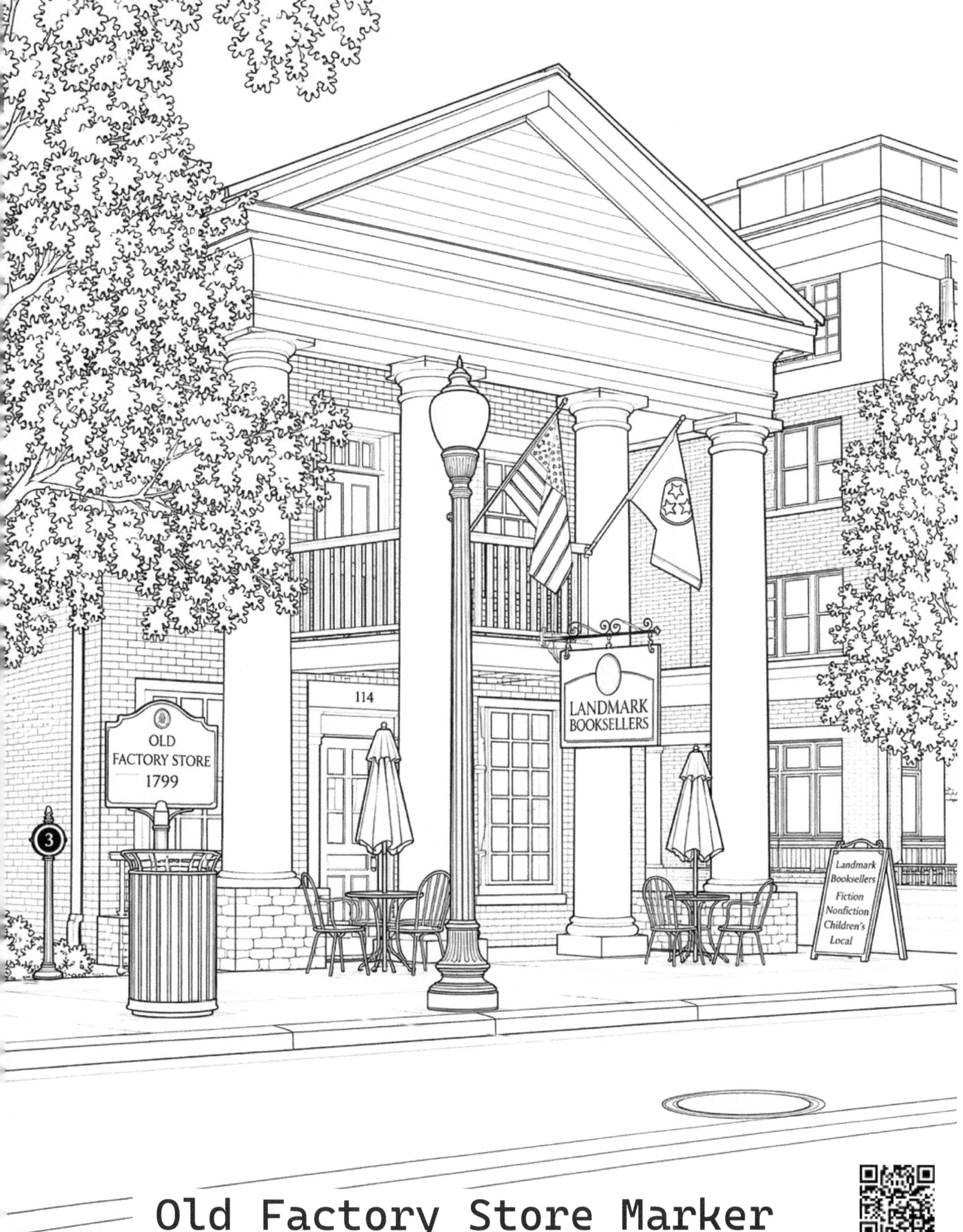

Old Factory Store Marker

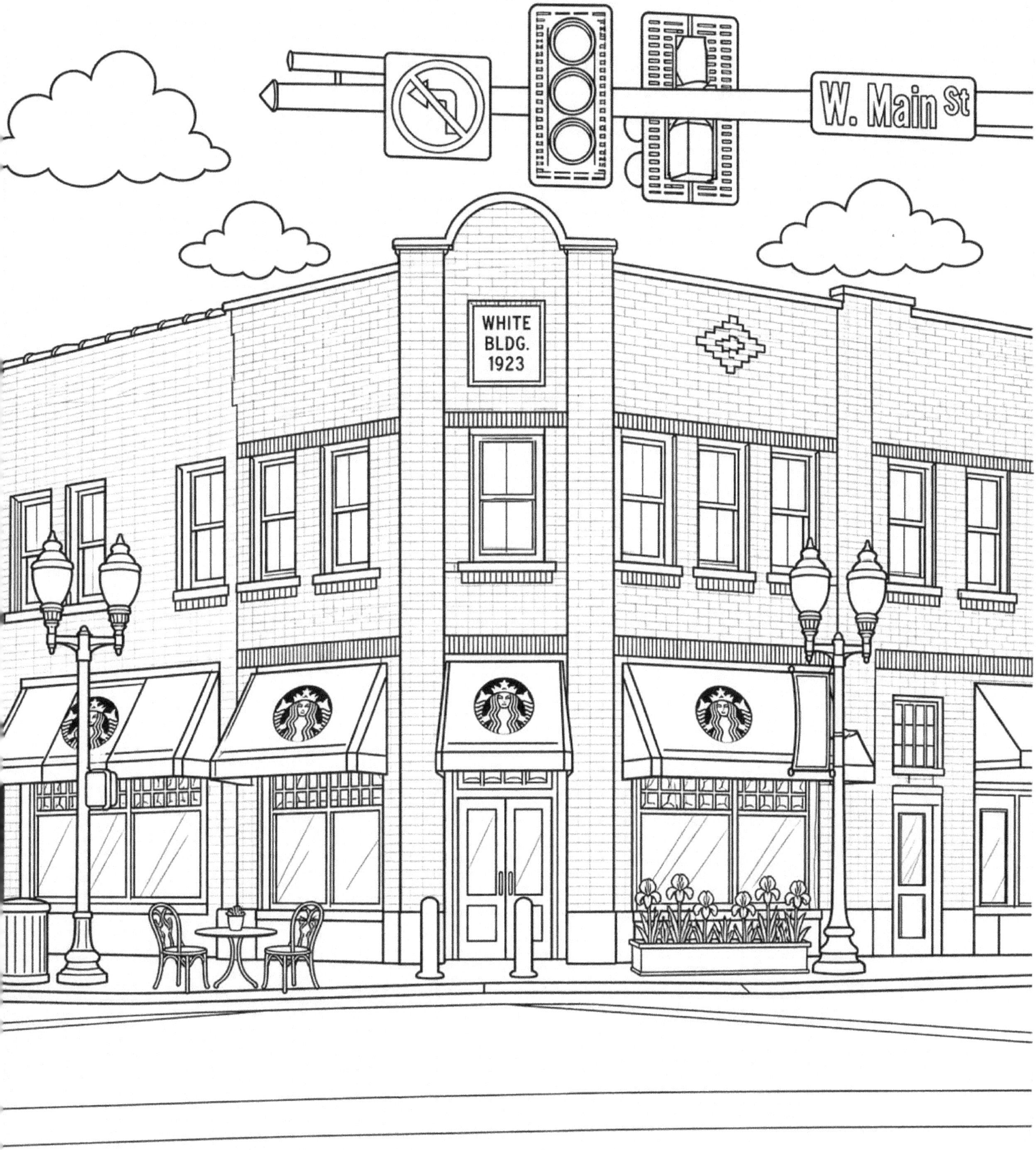

White Building 1923

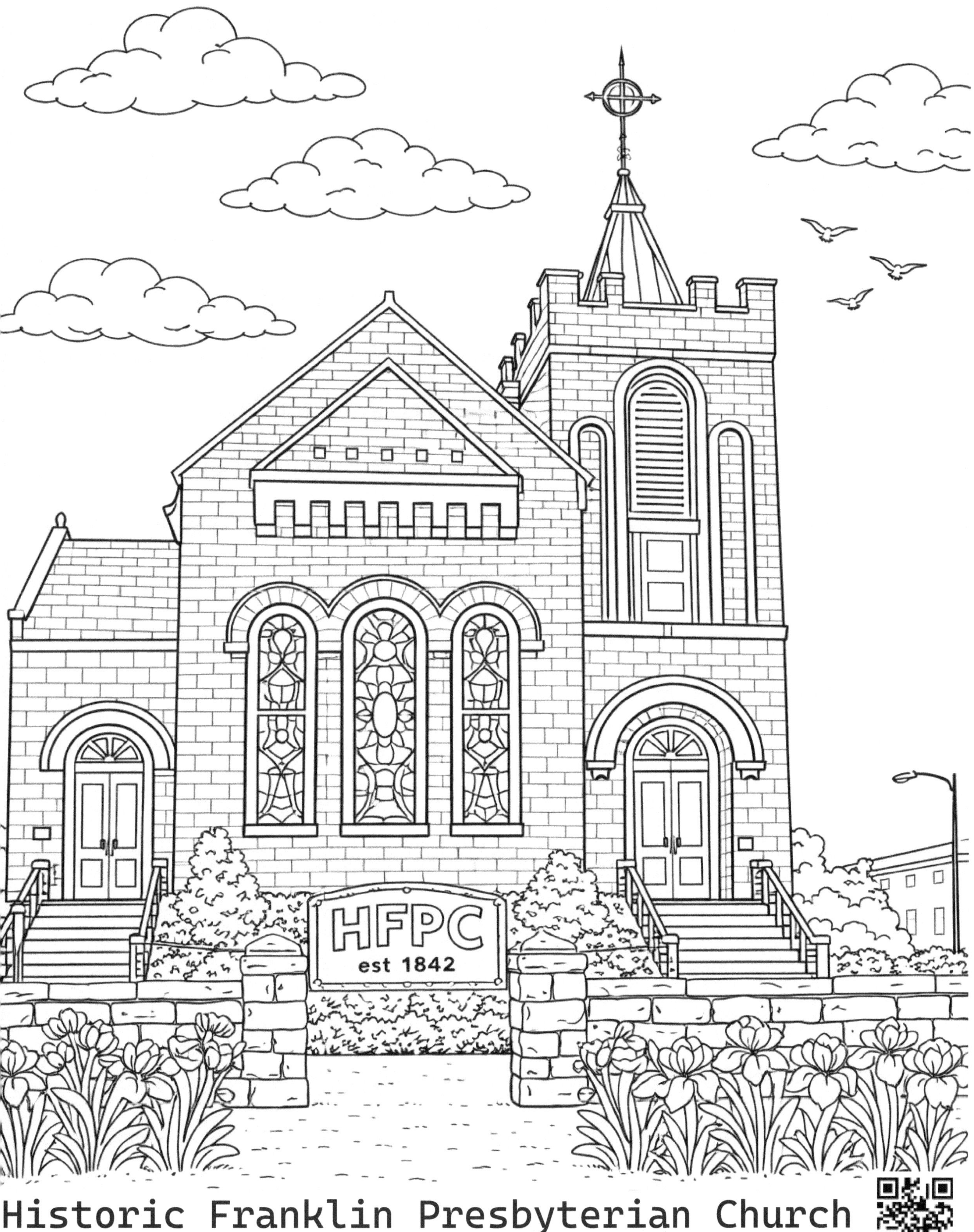

Historic Franklin Presbyterian Church

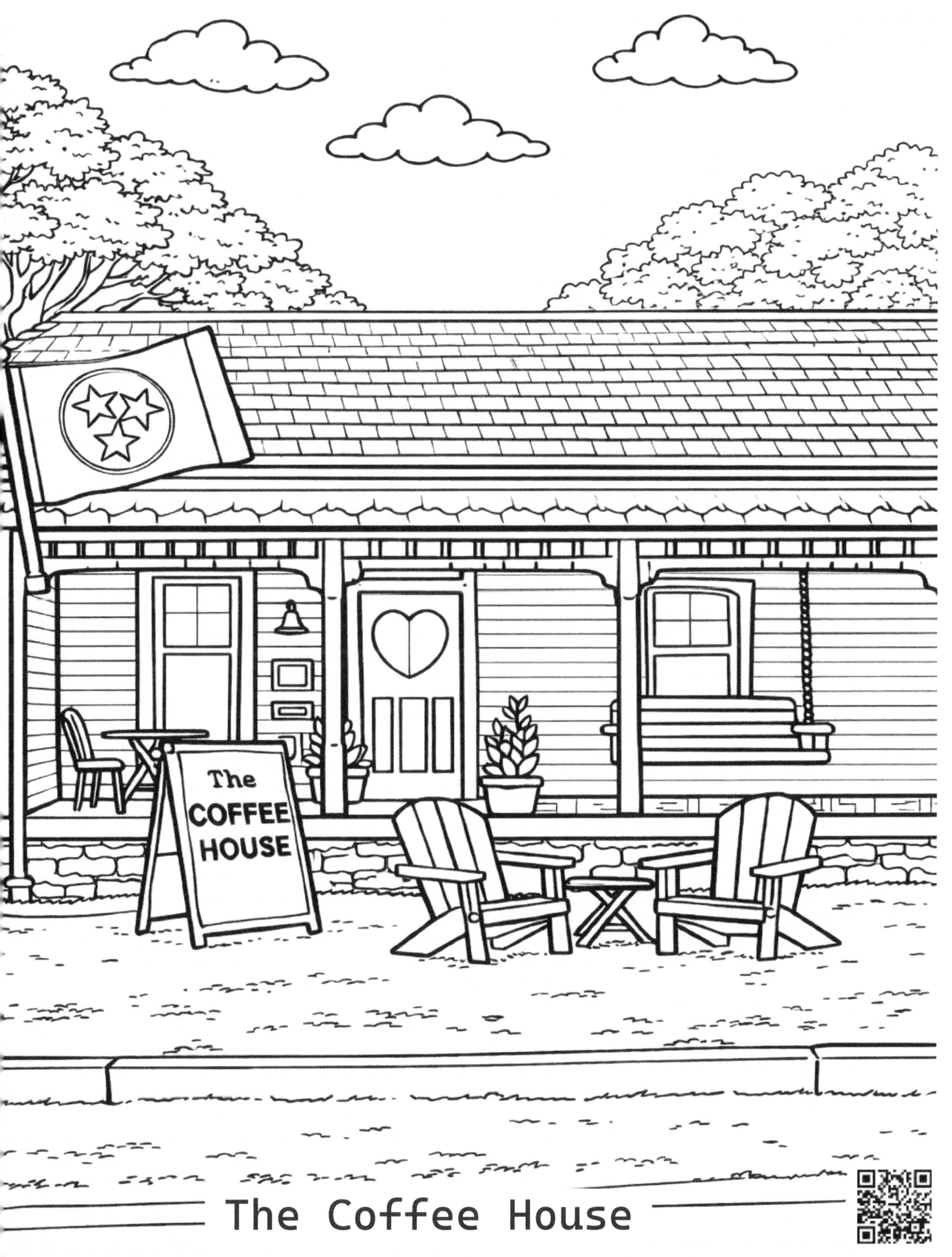

The Coffee House

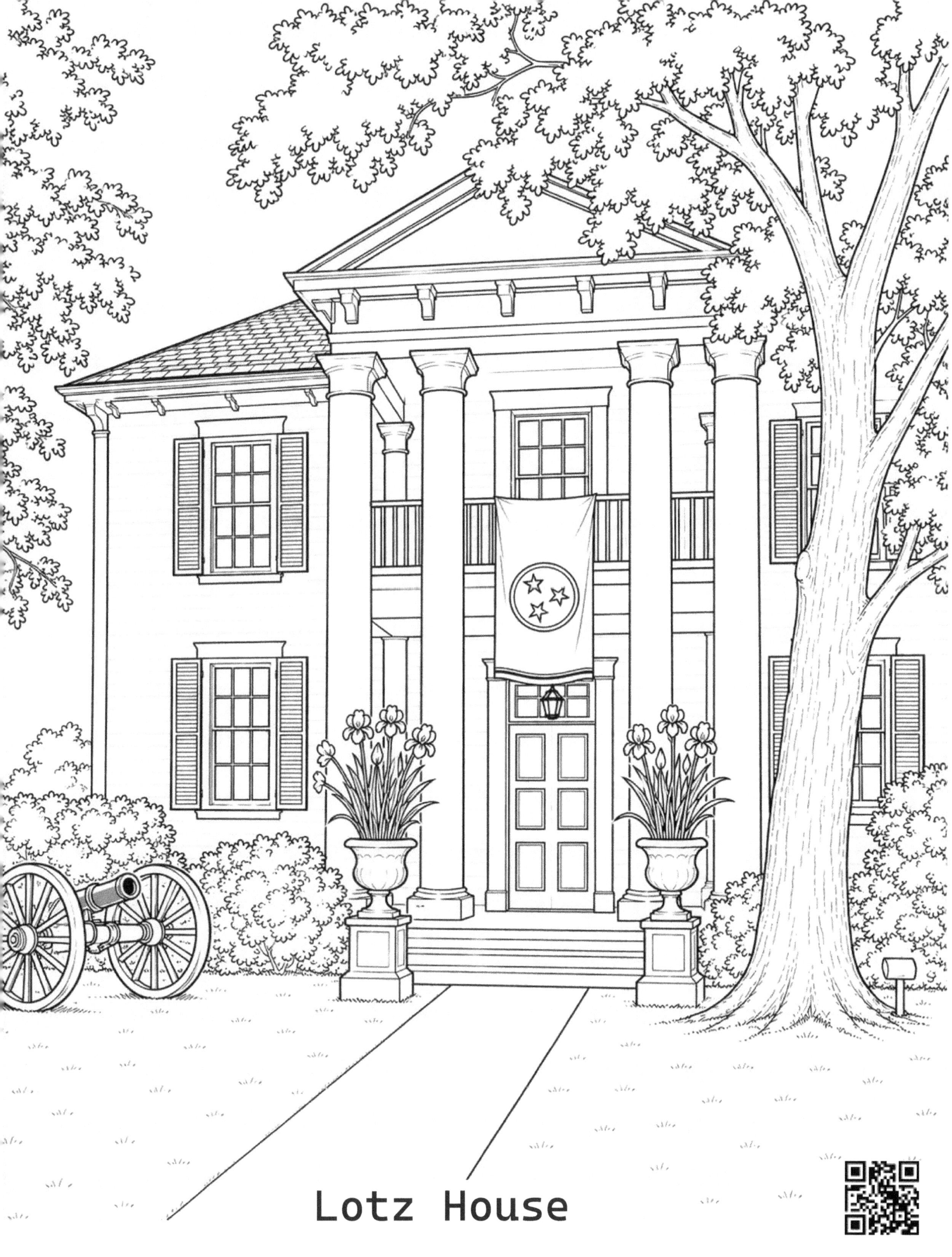

Lotz House

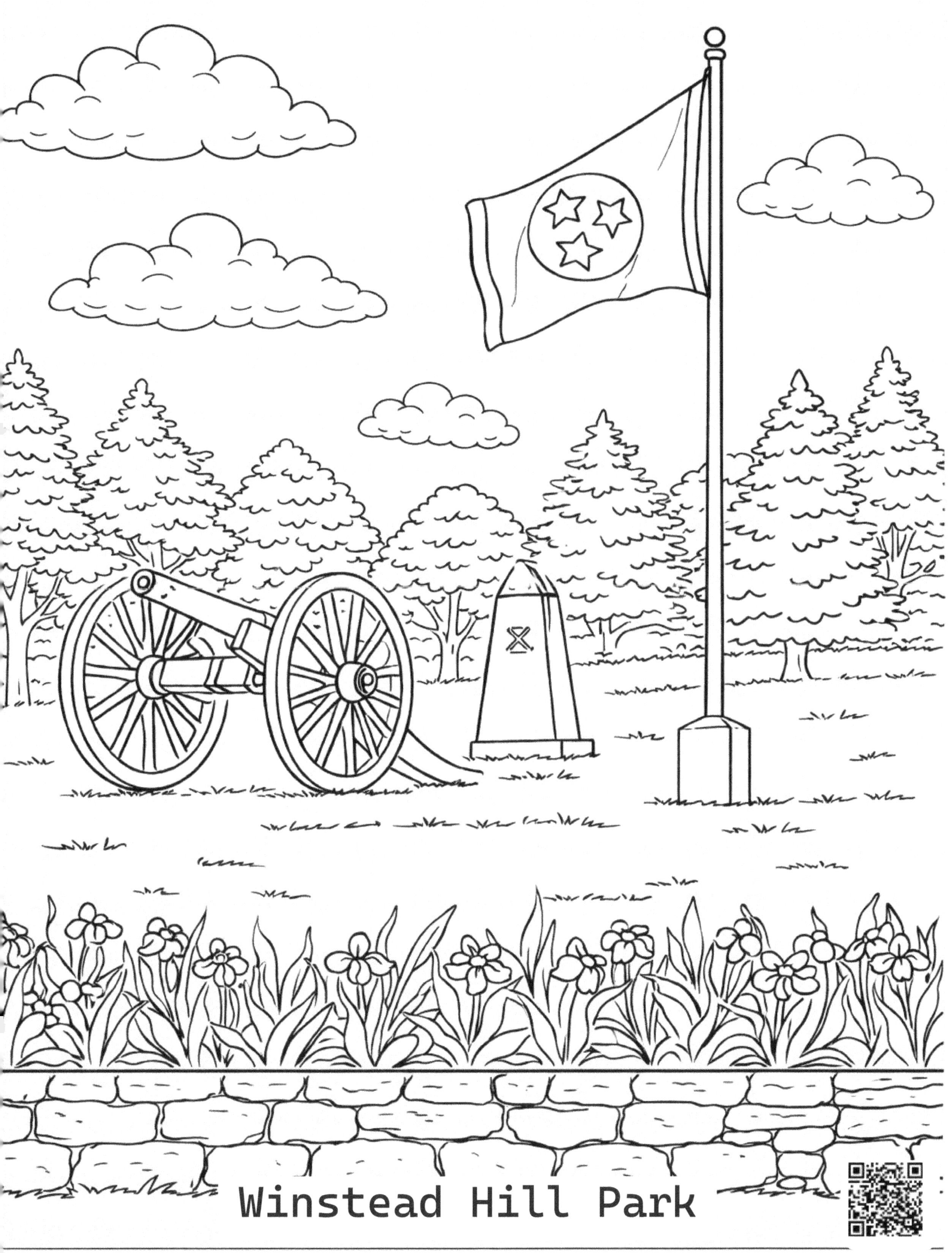

Winstead Hill Park

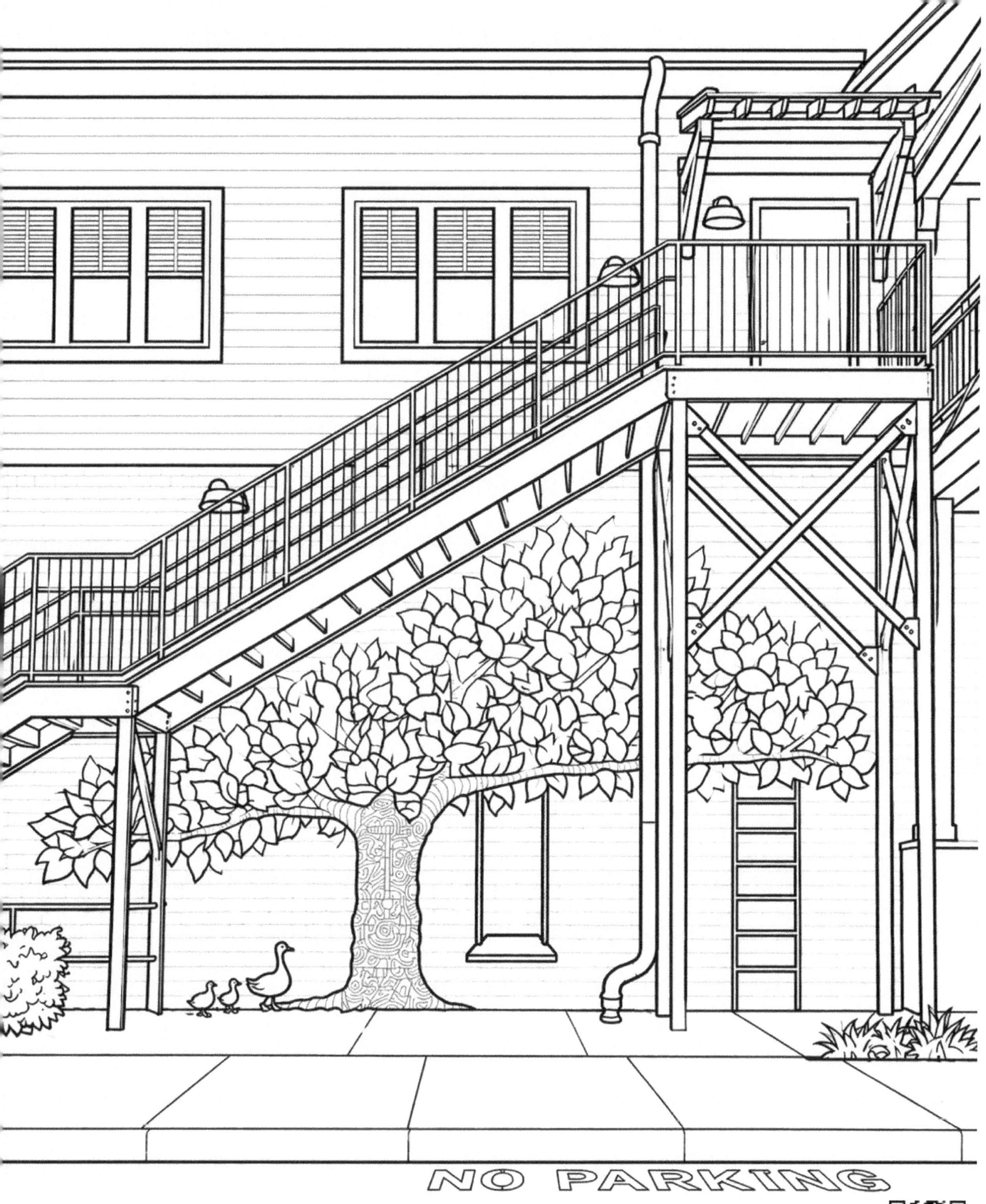

Westhaven Mural

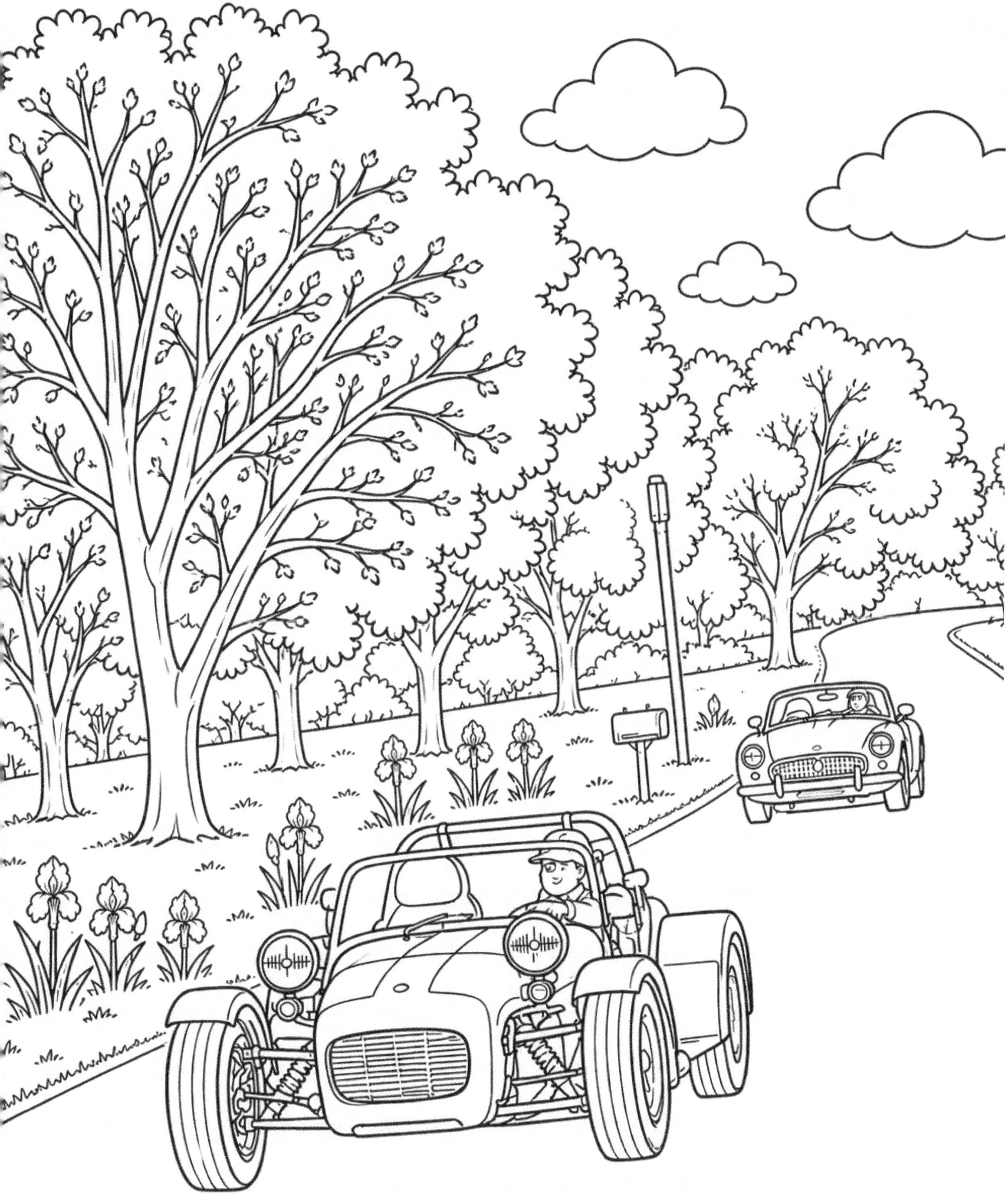

Franklin Traffic

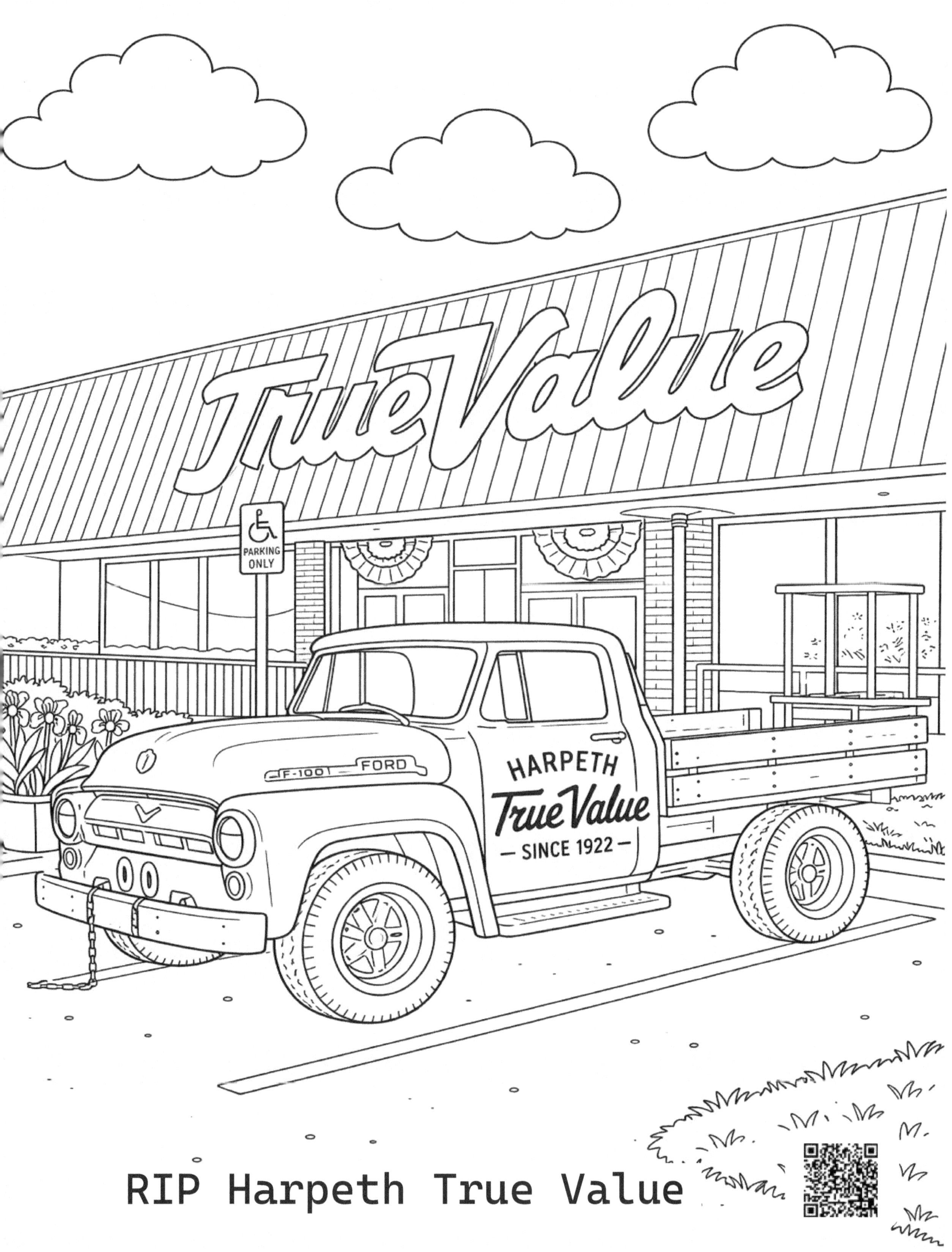

RIP Harpeth True Value

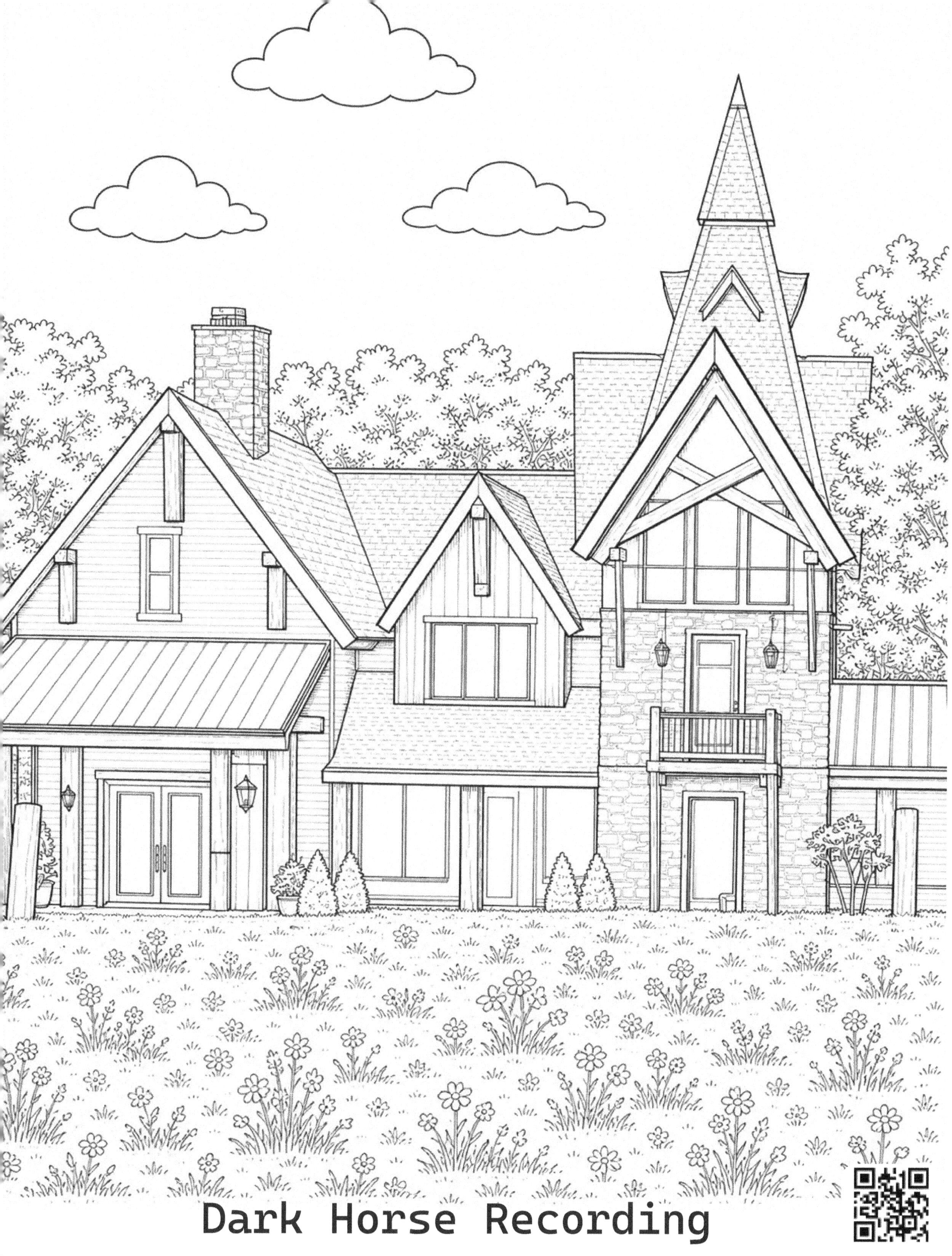

Dark Horse Recording

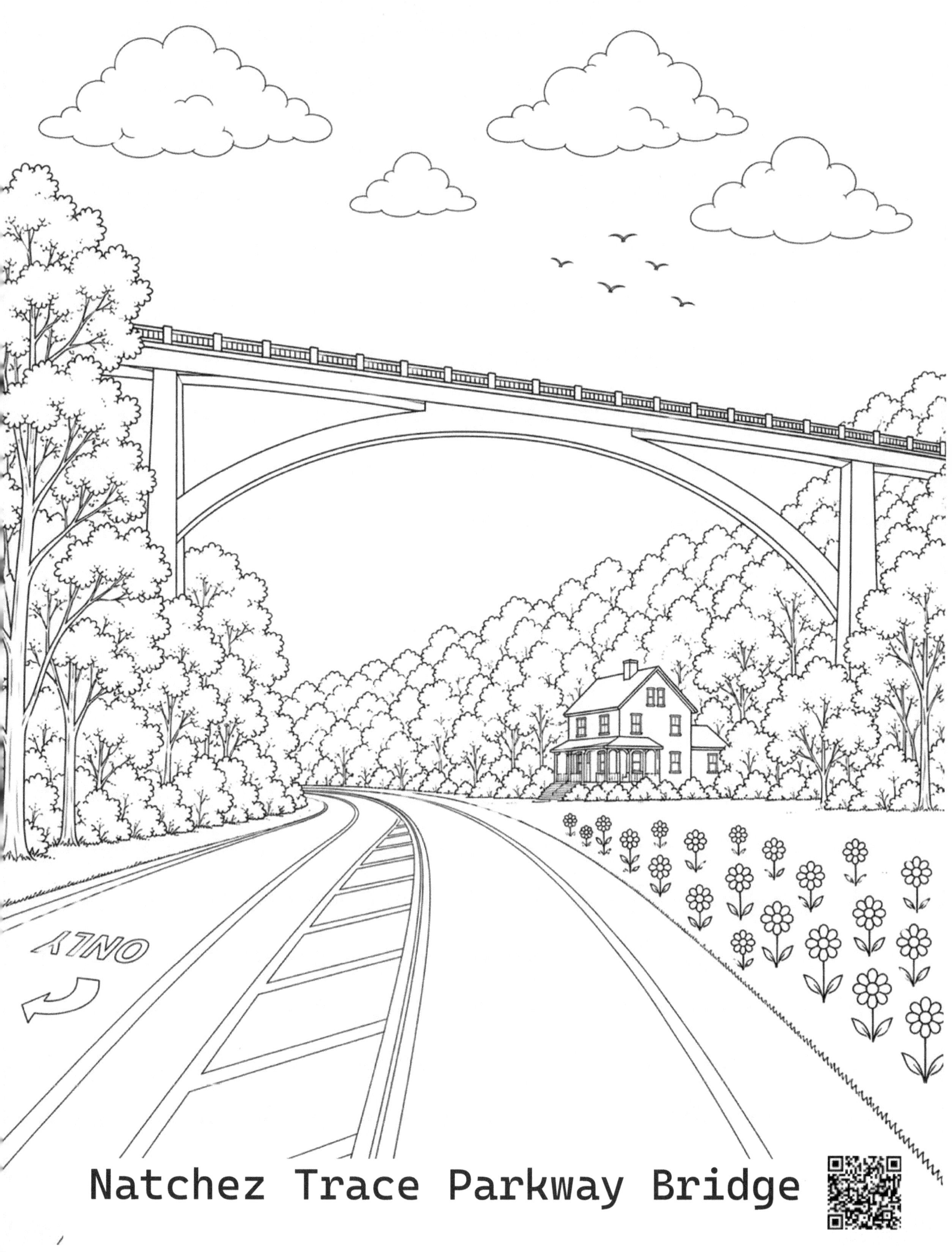

Natchez Trace Parkway Bridge

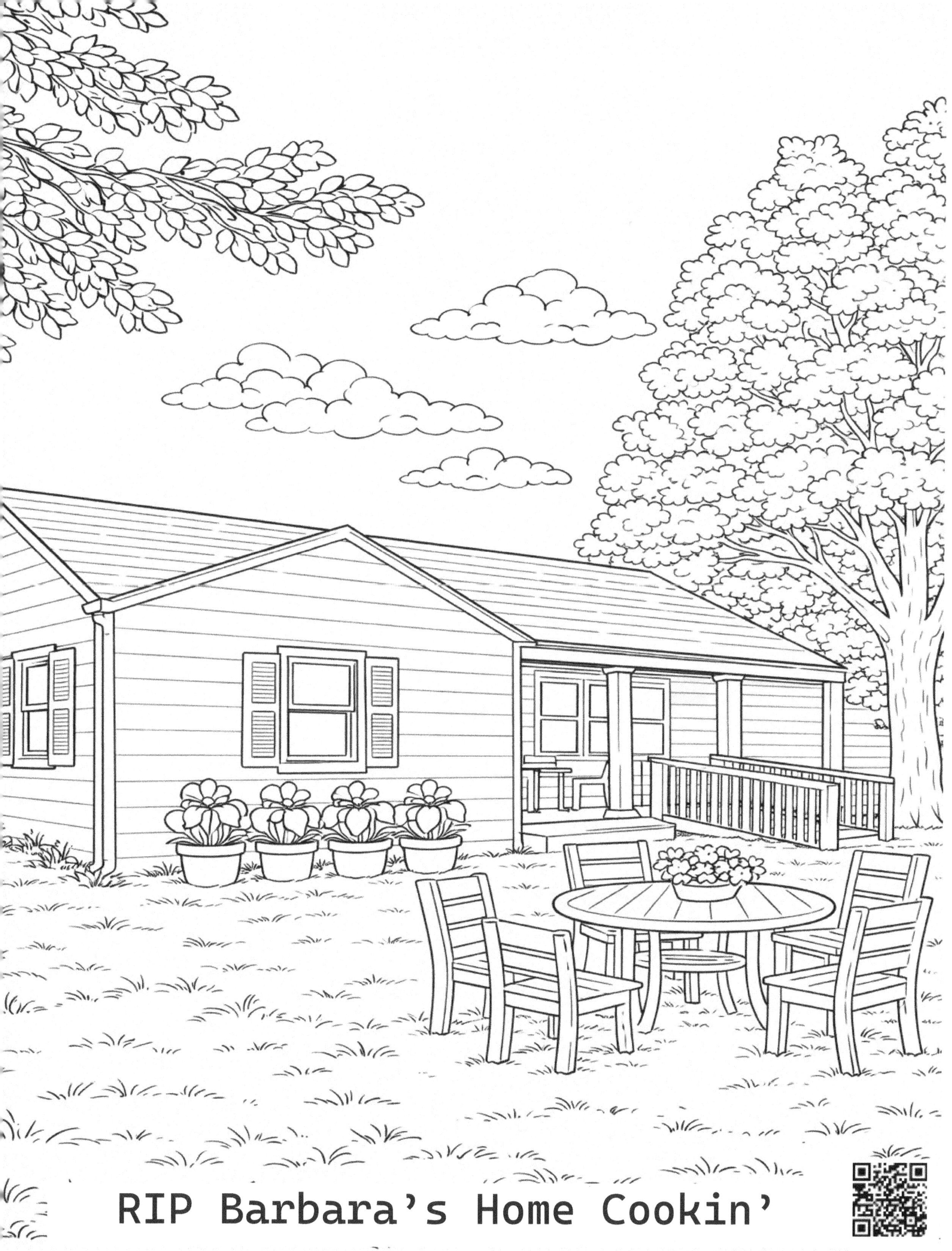

RIP Barbara's Home Cookin'

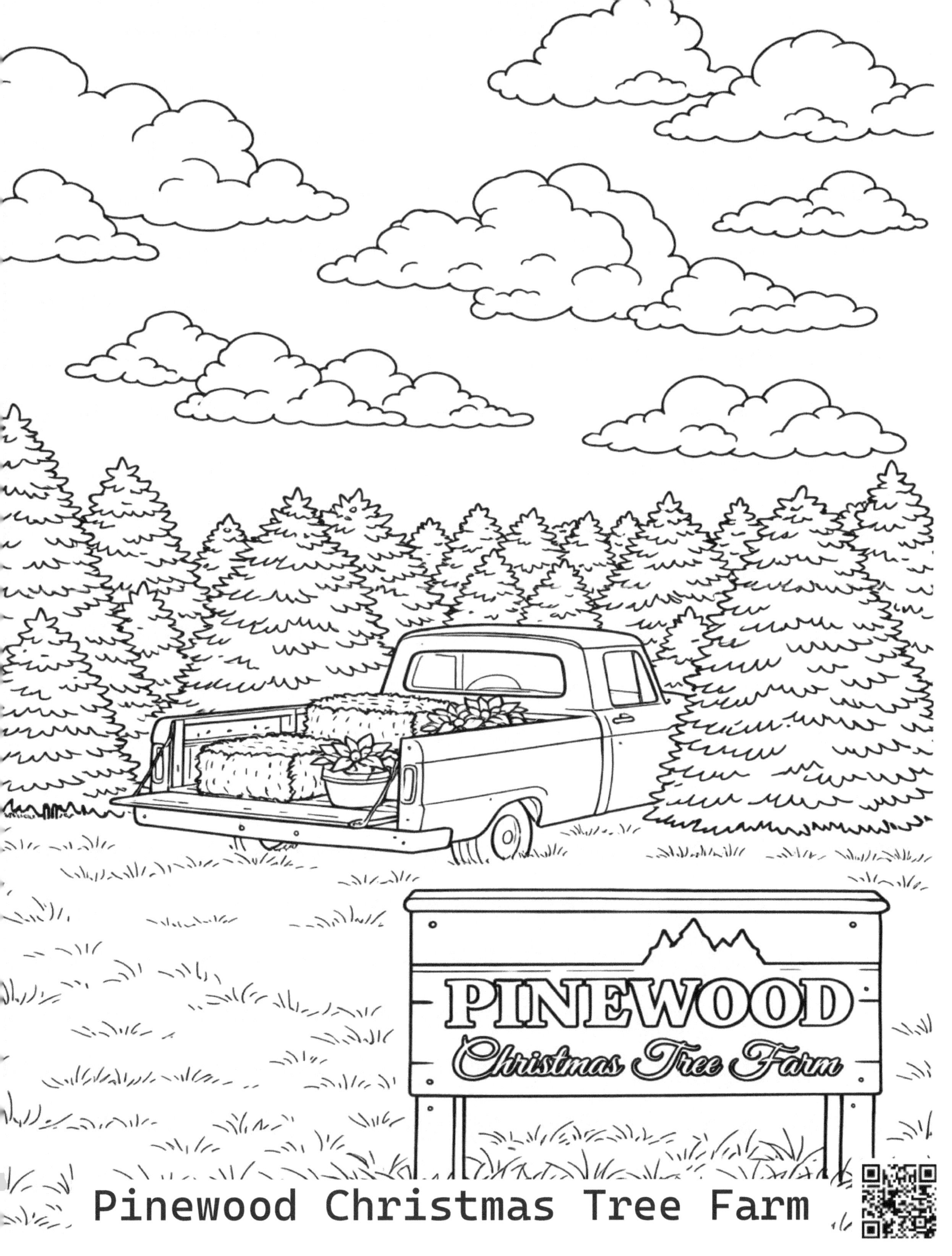

Pinewood Christmas Tree Farm

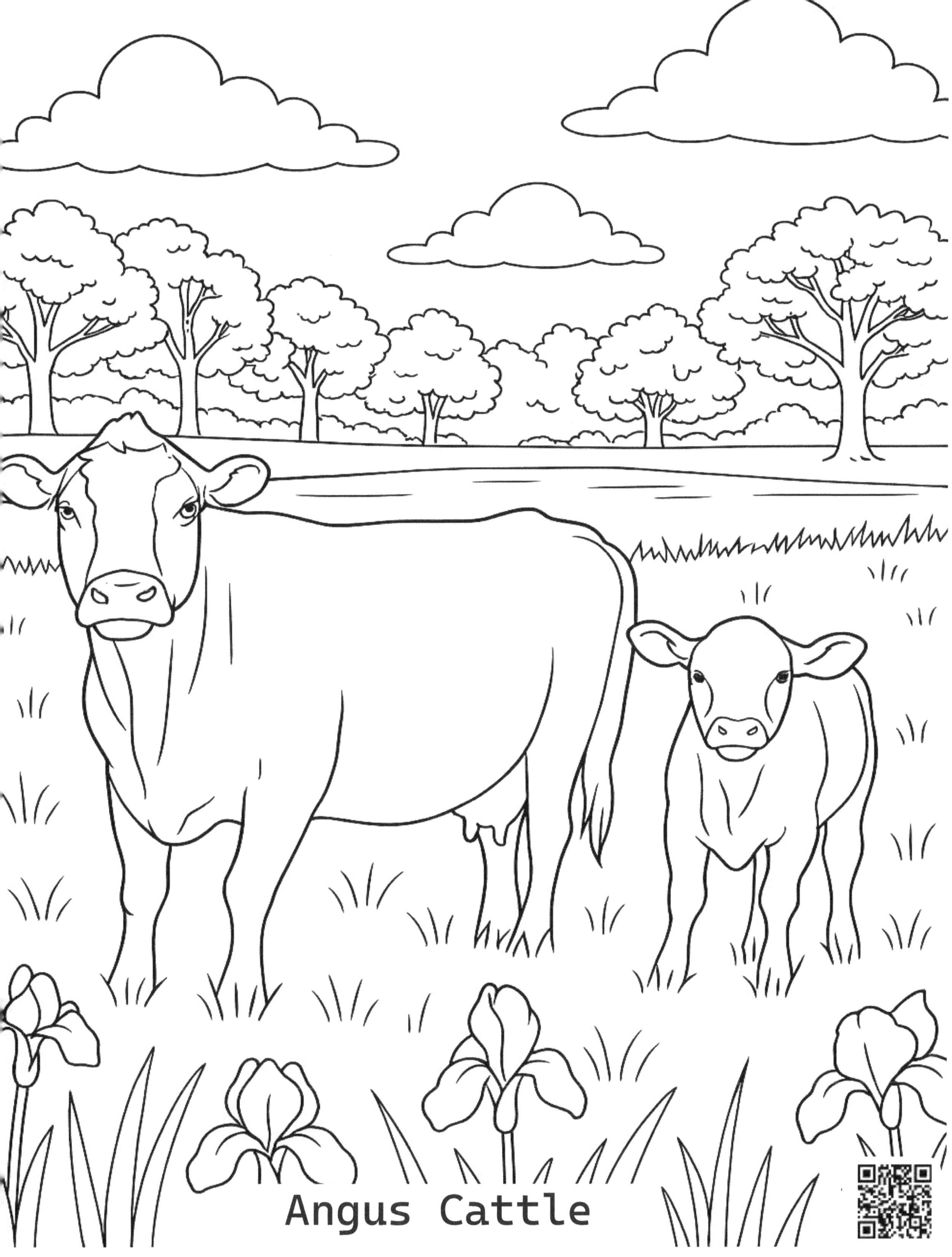

Angus Cattle

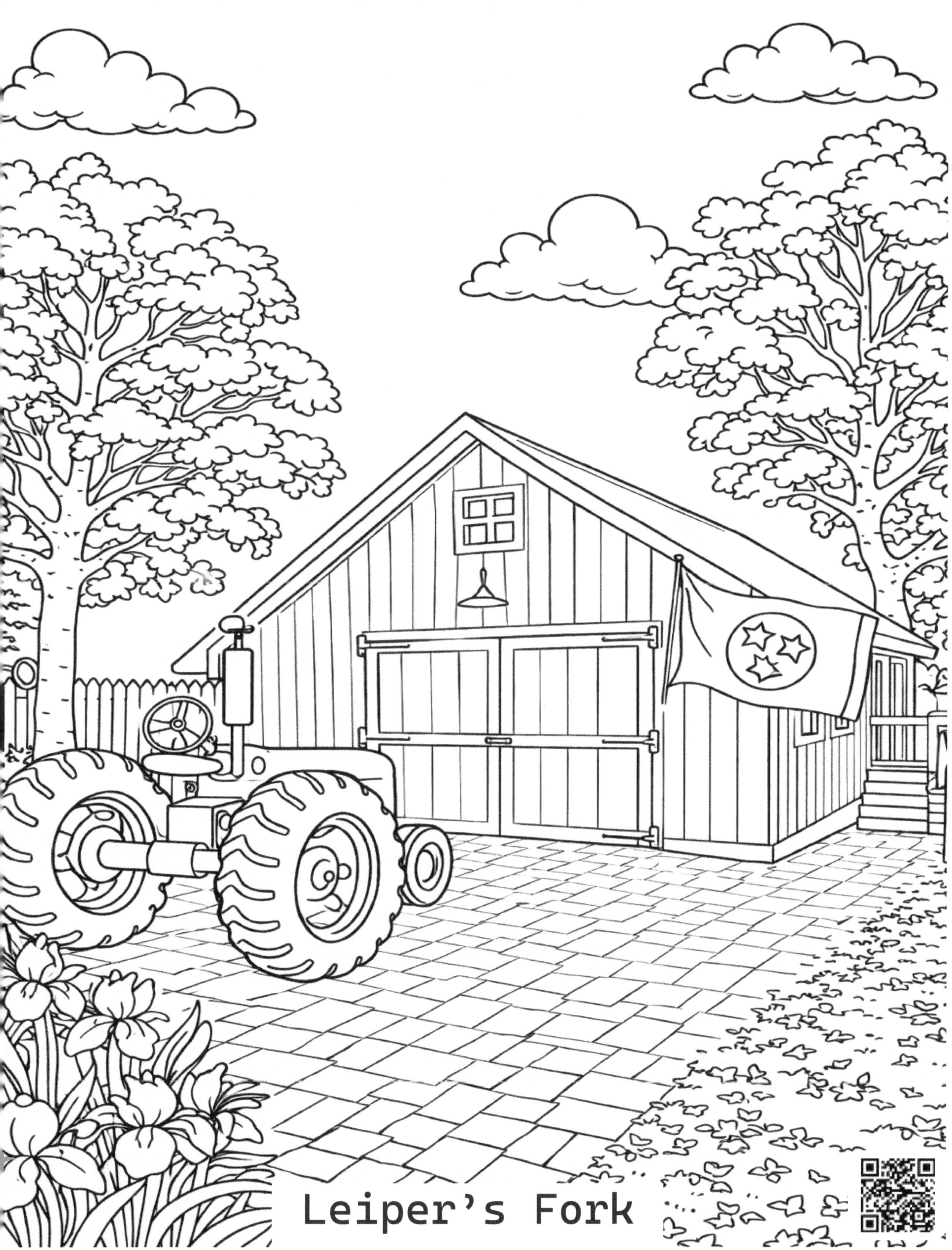
Leiper's Fork

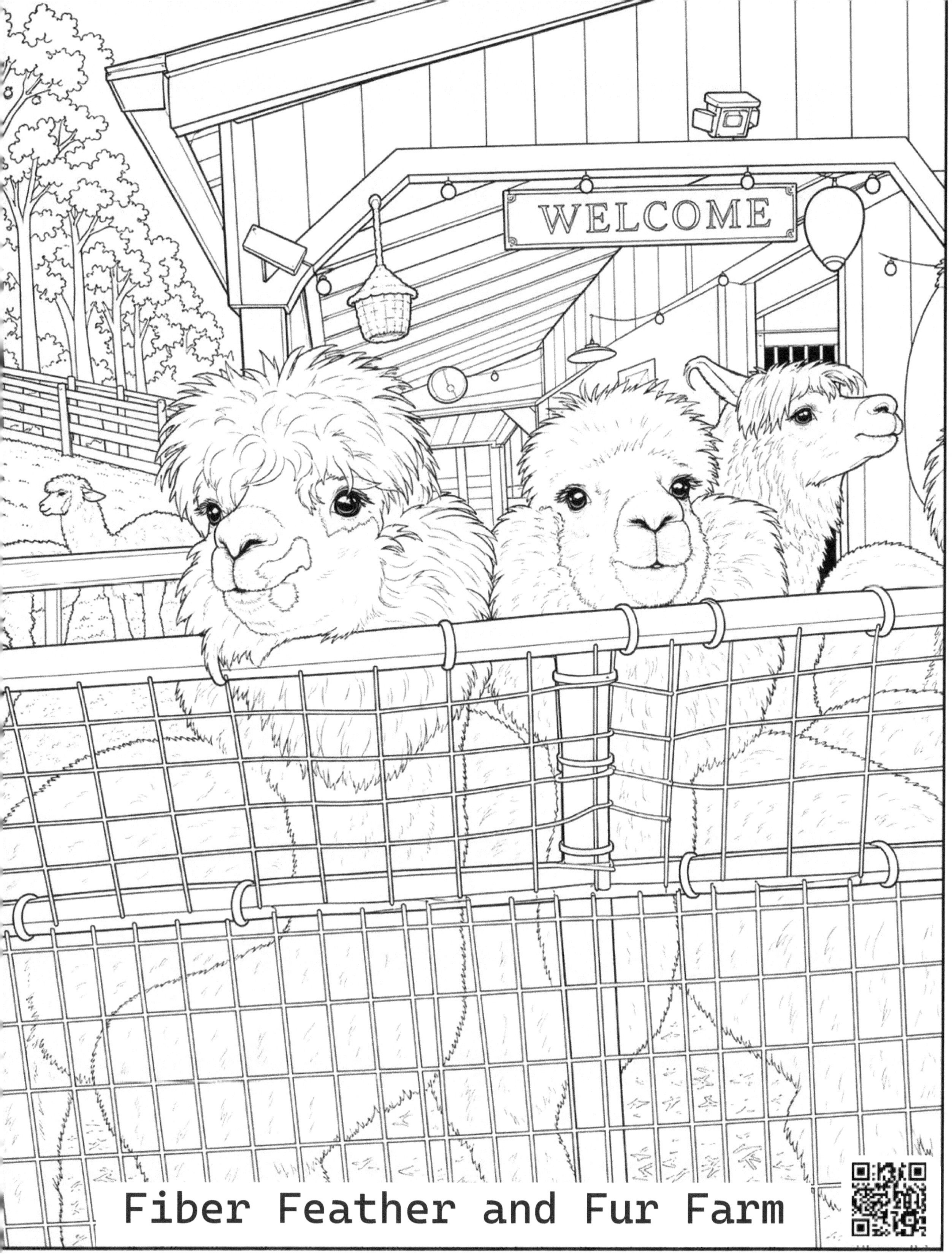

Fiber Feather and Fur Farm

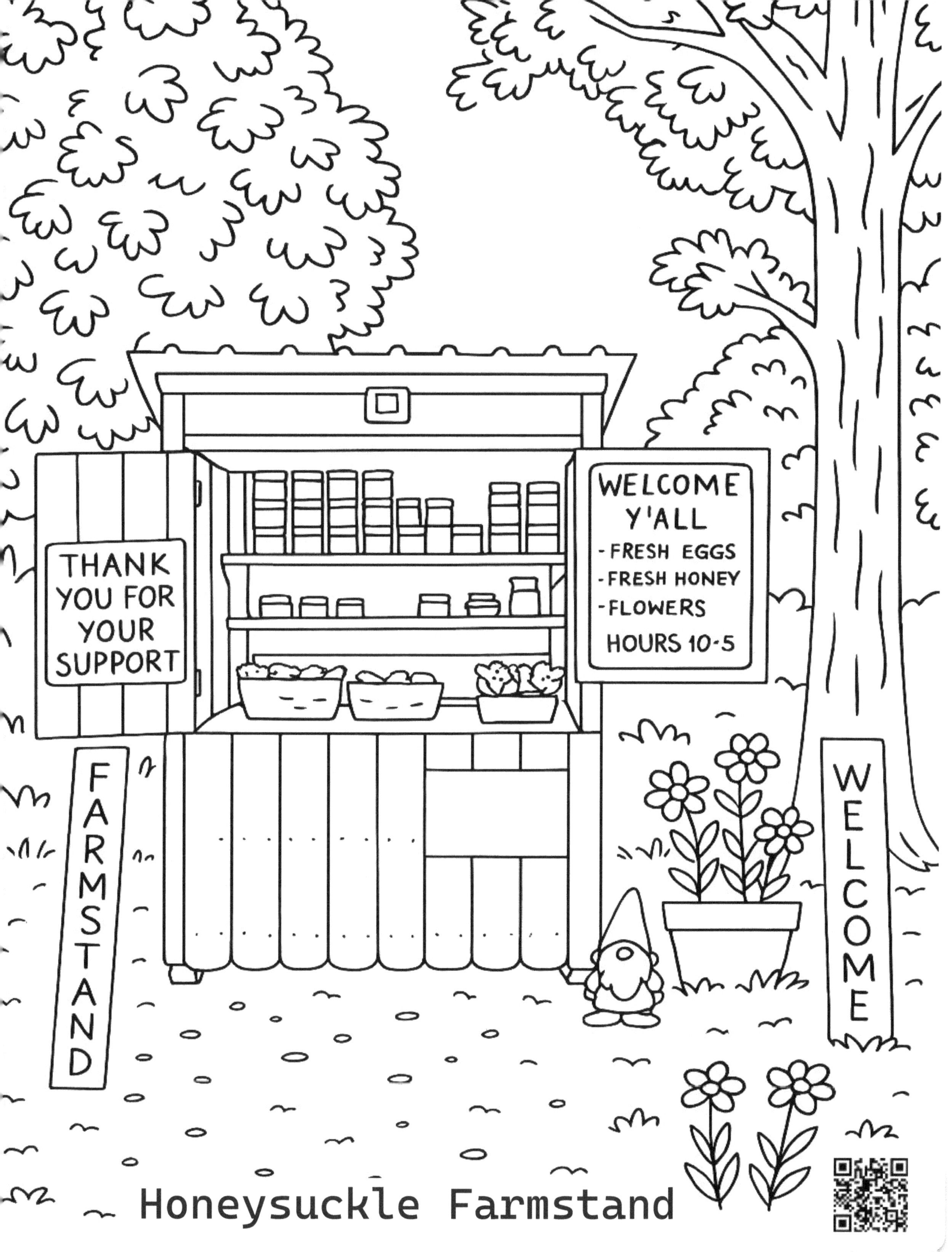

THANK YOU FOR YOUR SUPPORT
WELCOME Y'ALL
- FRESH EGGS
- FRESH HONEY
- FLOWERS
HOURS 10-5
FARMSTAND
WELCOME
Honeysuckle Farmstand

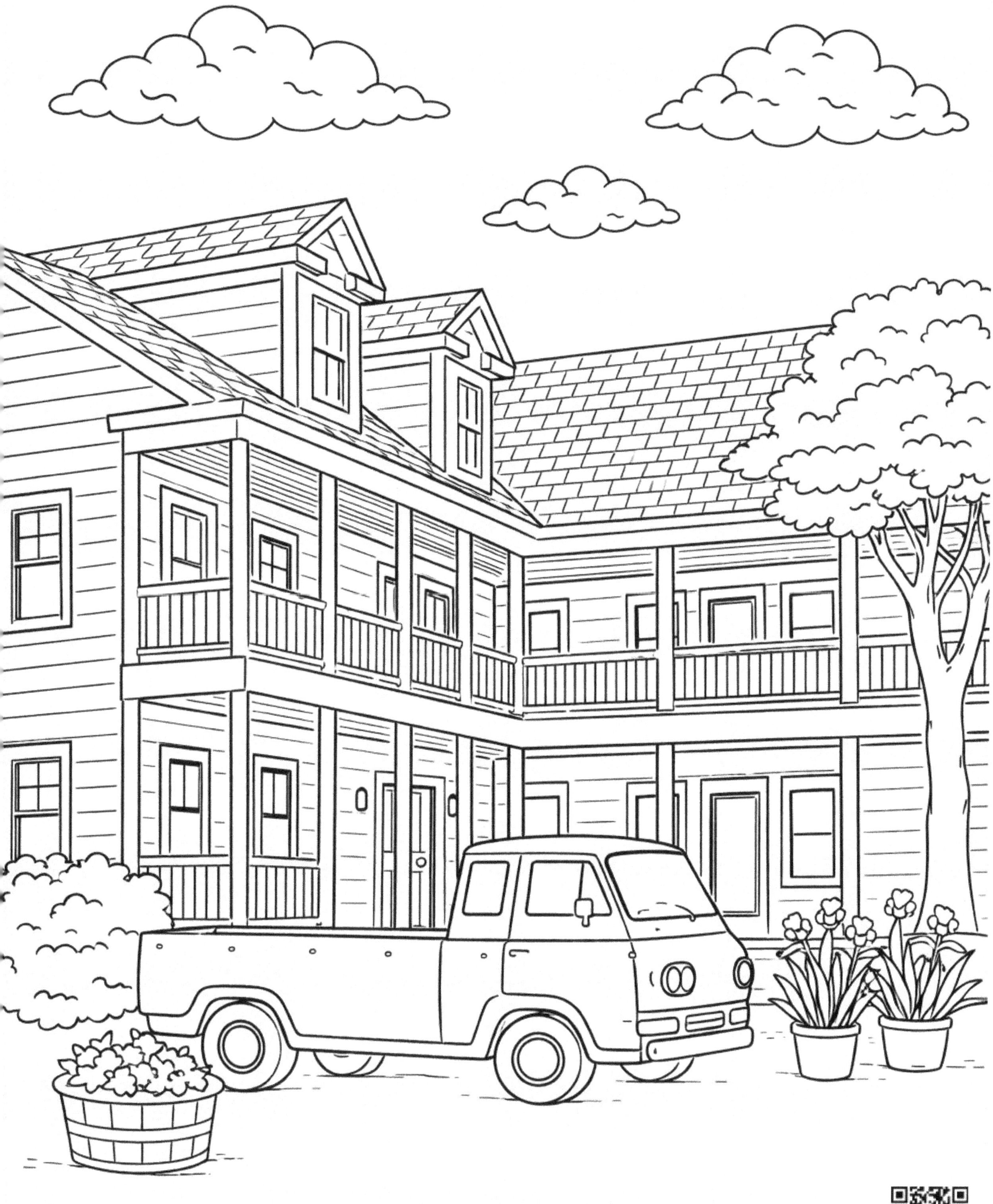

Leiper's Fork

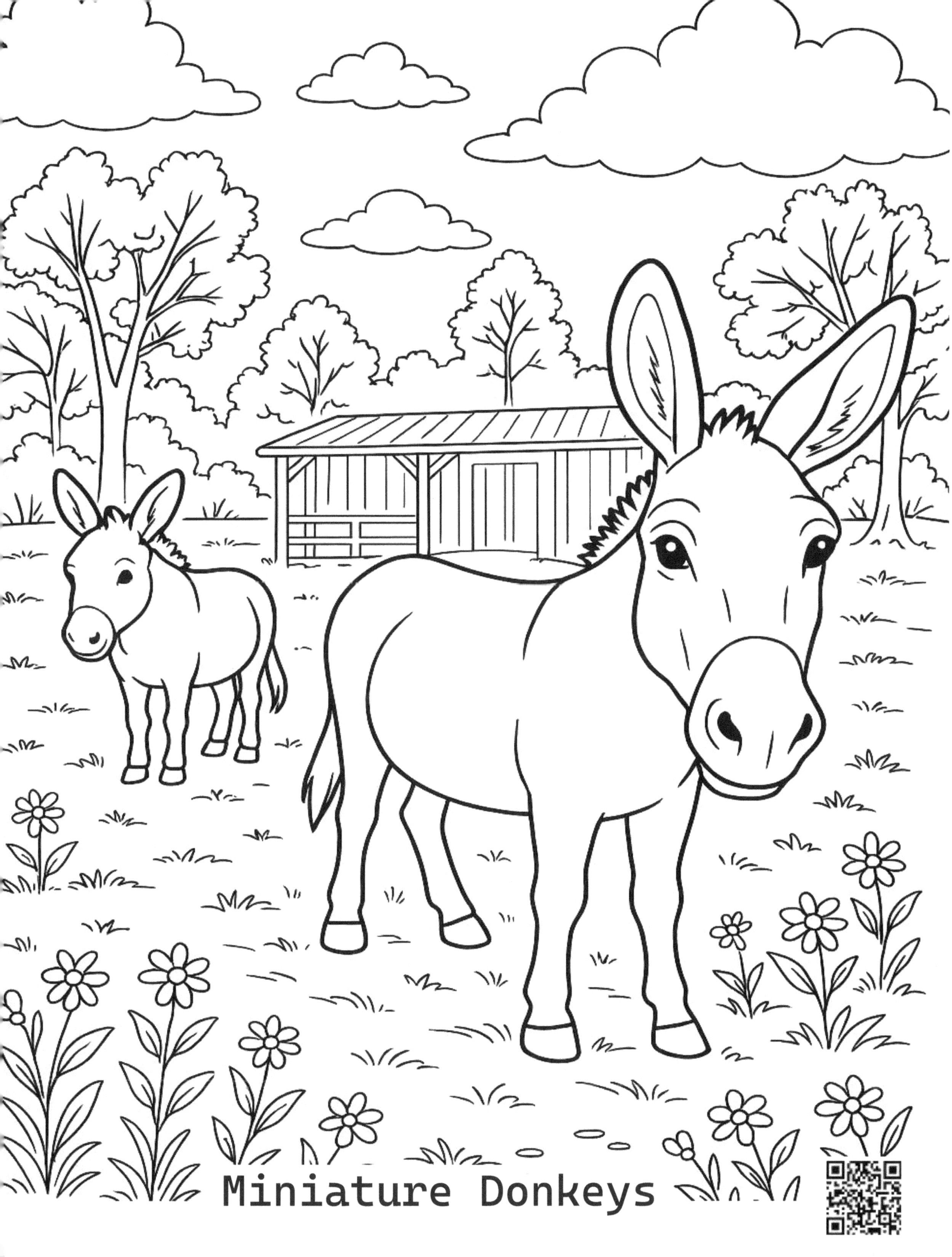
Miniature Donkeys

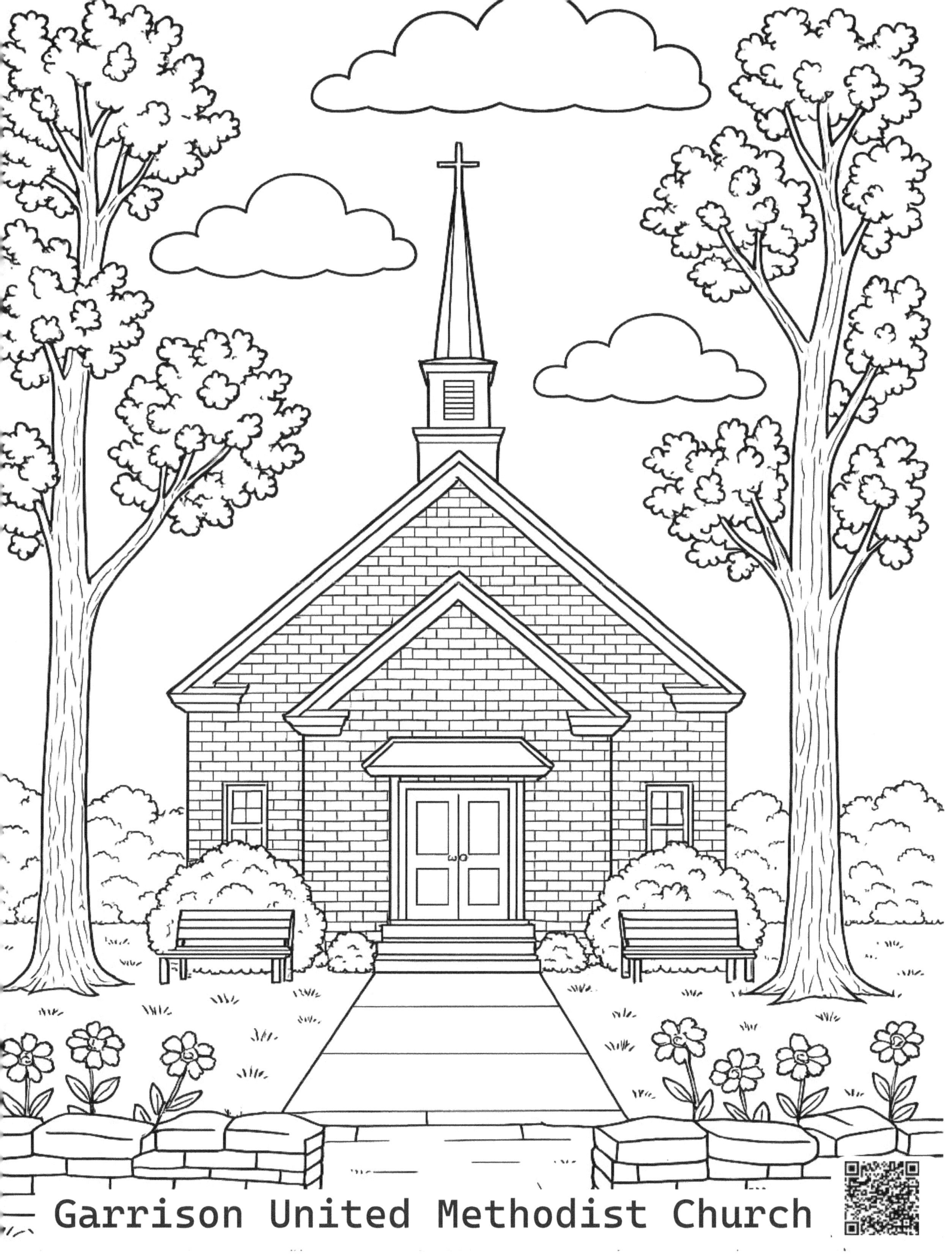

Garrison United Methodist Church

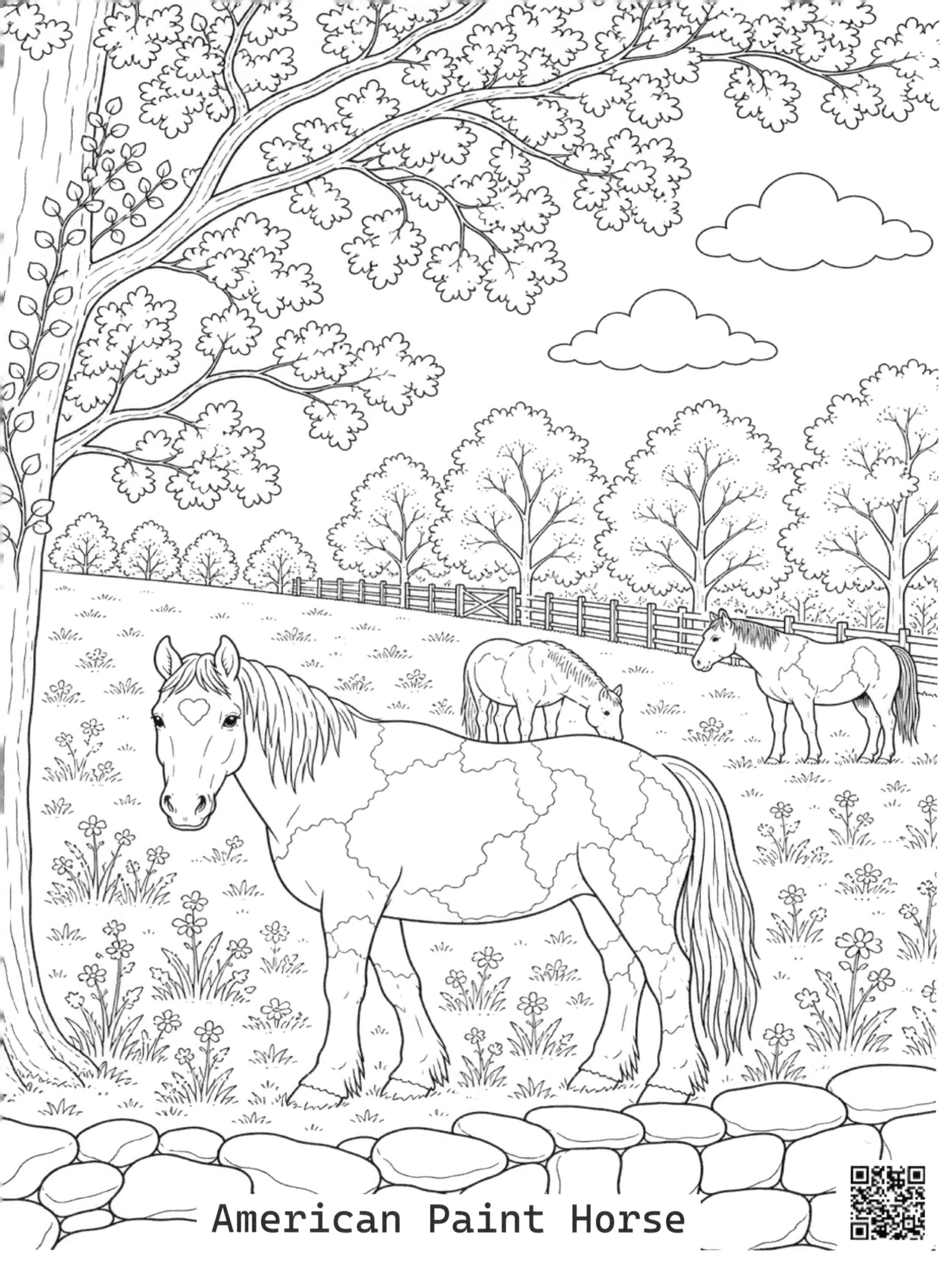

American Paint Horse

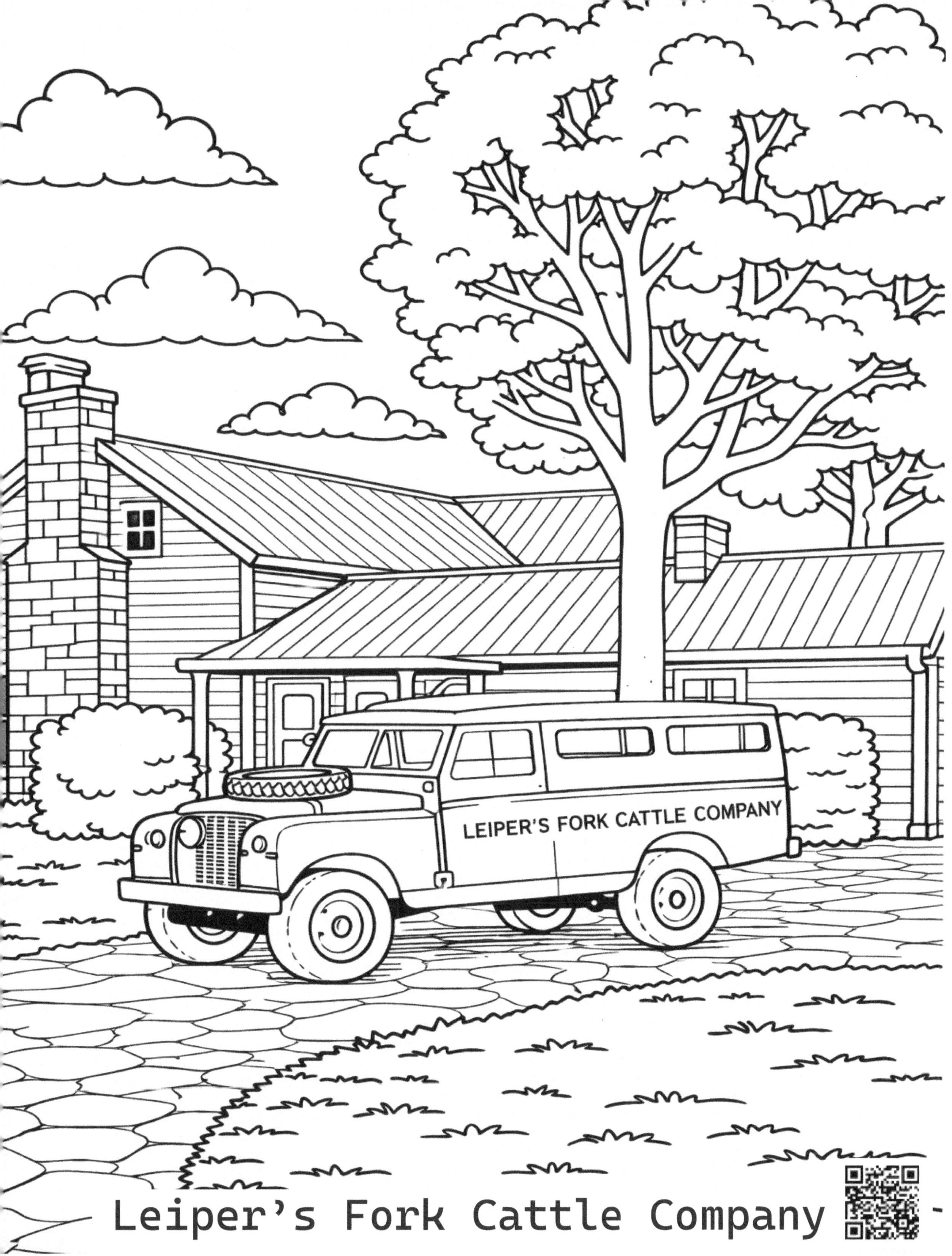

Leiper's Fork Cattle Company

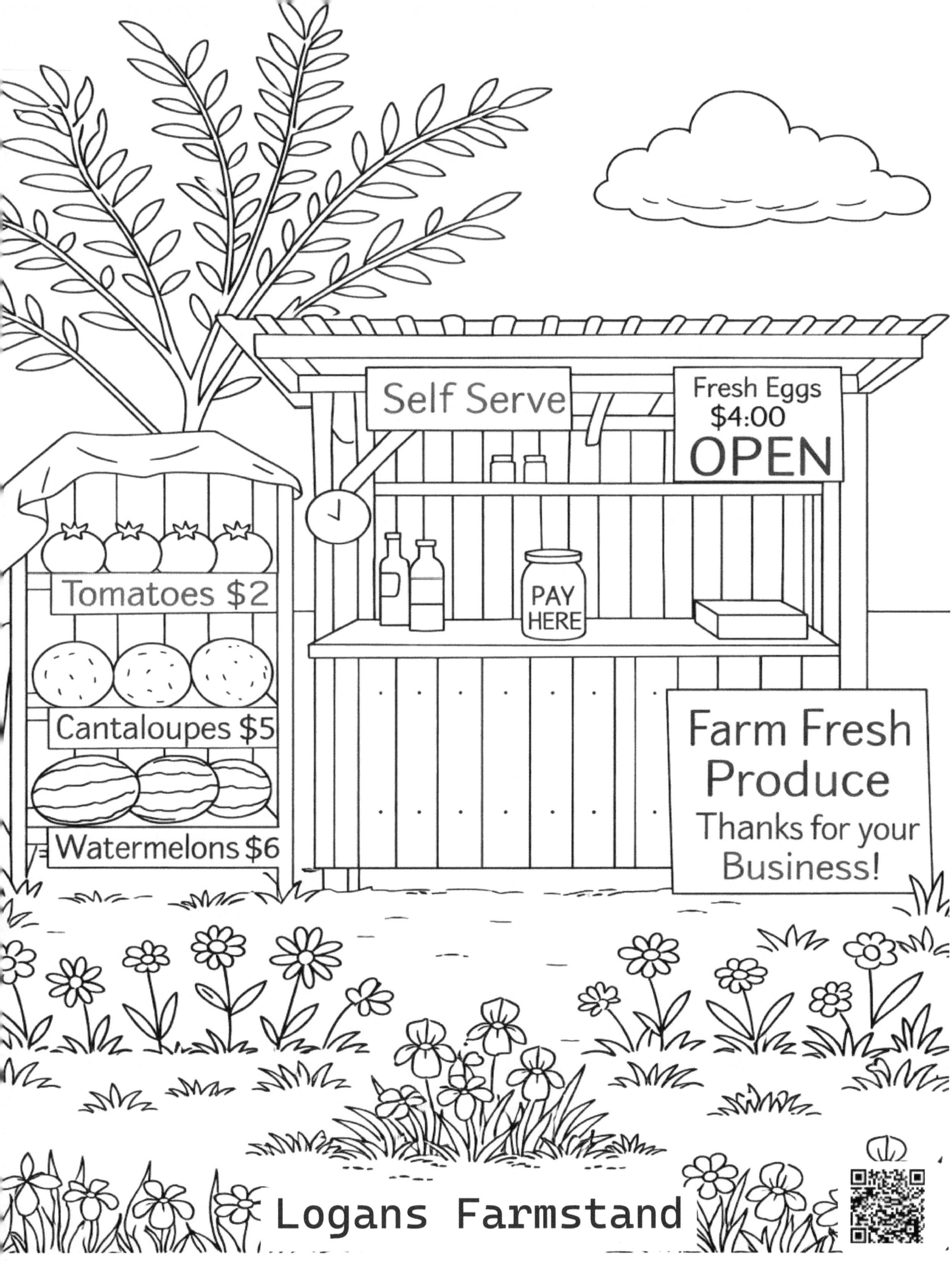

Self Serve
Fresh Eggs
$4:00
OPEN
Tomatoes $2
Cantaloupes $5
Watermelons $6
PAY HERE
Farm Fresh
Produce
Thanks for your
Business!
Logans Farmstand

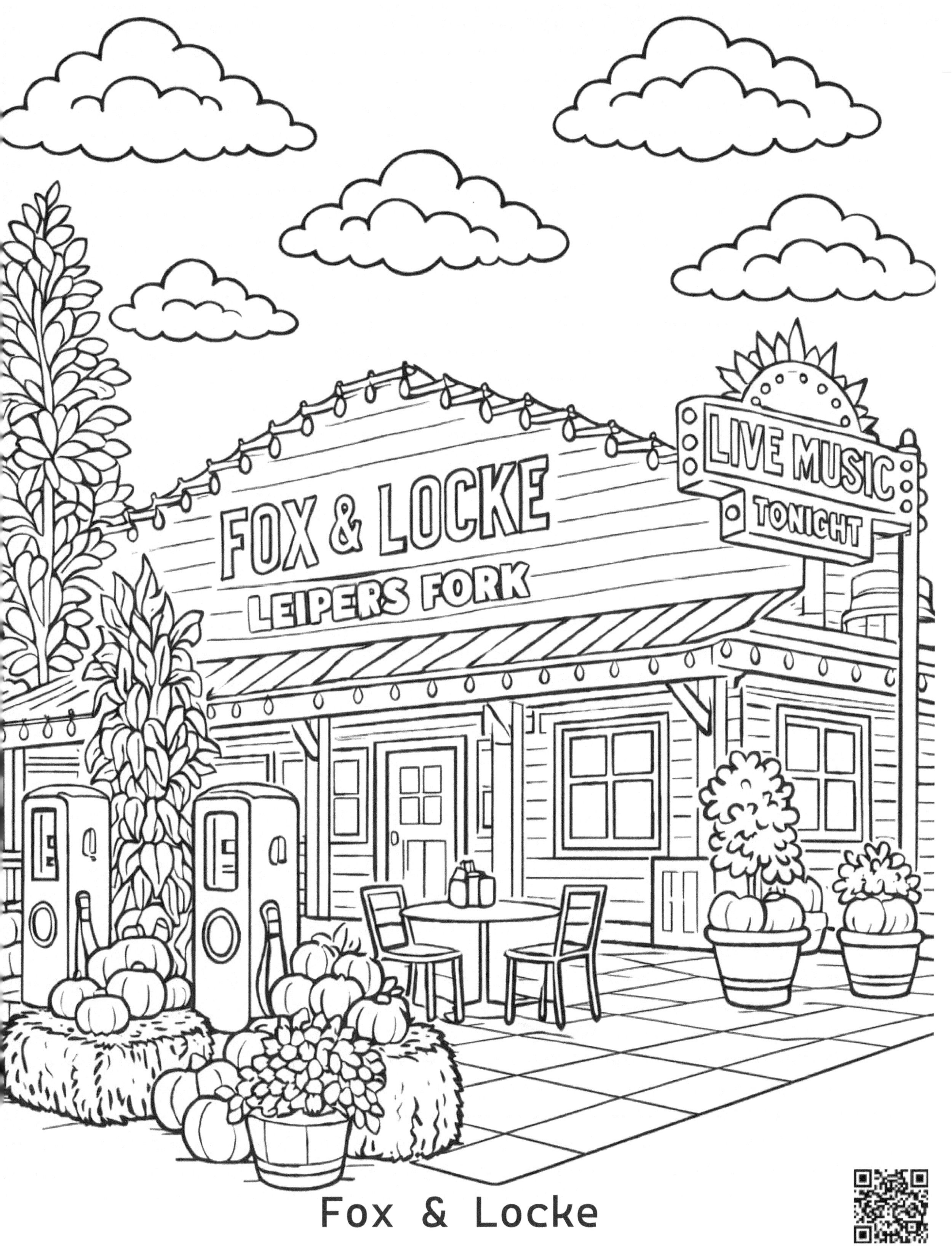

Fox & Locke